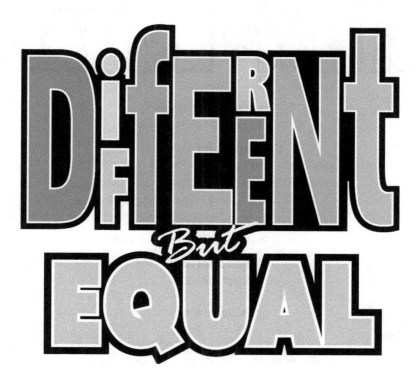

Teens Write About Living With Disabilities

By Youth Communication

Edited by Virginia Vitzthum

Read. Write. Succeed.

D1128076

EXECUTIVE EDITORS
Keith Hefner and Laura Longhine

CONTRIBUTING EDITORS
Philip Kay, Katia Hetter, Andrea Estepa, Nora McCarthy,
Tamar Rothenberg, Sean Chambers, Al Desetta,
Marie Glancey, and Hope Vanderberg

LAYOUT & DESIGN
Efrain Reyes, Jr. and Jeff Faerber

PRODUCTION
Stephanie Liu

COVER ART
YC Art Dept.

For reprint information, please contact Youth Communication.

ISBN 978-1-935552-32-1

Second, Expanded Edition

Printed in the United States of America

Youth Communication ®
New York, New York
www.youthcomm.org

Catalog Item #YD-25

Table of Contents

Contents

Using the Book

Introduction

Most teens share a desire to fit in and seem "normal," as well as a need to assert their independence. Teens with disabilities are no different. They just face extra obstacles. They must navigate the world from a wheelchair, or with a learning, speech, or other disability—*and* convince their peers that they are "normal." They must struggle to gain independence while also addressing the need for extra help. And other people's ignorance can make them feel even more alone.

In this book, teens with disabilities write about their experiences moving toward independence, overcoming prejudice, and connecting with others. They are candid about their struggles, and provide valuable insight into how adults and peers can be supportive. Other teens write about the challenges of dealing with a disabled family member, or how getting to know people with disabilities widened their worldviews.

In "Facing Reality," Tania Morales describes the scary realization at age 13 that her legs are growing weaker. She is eventually diagnosed with a disease called Frederick's ataxia. She resists sitting in her new wheelchair as long as she can. Like many of the other writers in this book, Tania goes through a period of denial about her disability. And then, she writes, "After three years of not wanting to know about what I had, I realized I was curious, too. Besides, I wasn't getting better and it no longer seemed possible to ignore the effects of the disease." Researching Frederick's ataxia held some shocks, like finding out she was at risk for developing fatal heart problems. But it also made her more determined to seize the days she does have.

In "Getting the Words Out," Gamal Jones writes with good humor about the frustrations of having a stutter, including other kids' mockery and his own reluctance to speak at all. He shares unconventional solutions from his own family: "My grandmother yelled and demanded that my mother stop stuttering (her form of shock therapy). It worked. My brother got over his stuttering by listening to professionals on TV and mimicking them."

Gamal himself goes to speech therapy, where his homework is to read aloud, but he gets more help from his dad, who shares a breathing technique. "I had to sit with my eyes closed and breathe in and out according to a specific pattern, following along with African music. My dad guaranteed that if I practiced 30 minutes a day for a month or two, it would eventually eliminate my problem. And he was right."

In a companion article, Gamal interviews a stuttering expert, who explains what happens in the brain and vocal cords when a person stutters. Slade Anderson also supplements his personal story: In "What's It Like Being Blind?" he answers common questions people ask about his condition. To the question "How do you go to the bathroom?" he replies, "I walk up to the toilet until my shins hit the edge and then move back a couple steps." To the question, "How do blind people deal with money?" he answers, "I fold all my bills differently. I fold my $20 bills like a triangle and my $10 bills like a square."

Too often, able-bodied people avoid people with disabilities because they're afraid of saying or doing the wrong thing. In these stories, simple information is often the answer to those fears. In "Classmate in a Wheelchair," Esther Rajavelu charts her own progress from ignoring a disabled student to working up the nerve to talk to him. "I tried to be very honest about my feelings and stereotypes, and I asked a lot of questions. I think it paid off, because my attitude began to change a little," she writes.

With its first-person accounts and straightforward answers to uncomfortable questions, this book can help dispel similar fears in teens who are uncertain about how to deal with disabled peers. And these stories show disabled teens that they are not alone in the challenges in they face.

The names in *My Sister's Keeper* have been changed.

Patricia Battles

The Art of Shotokan

By Otis Hampton

I was born with cerebral palsy (CP), which limits my movements. One of my legs is stronger than the other, so I'm not able to kick as high or run as fast as most people. In 10th grade, I was taken out of regular gym class and put in a class for kids with disabilities and special education students.

I never liked gym class, which was usually spent playing basketball. I was surprised and excited when the teacher told the class that we'd be doing martial arts. I imagined chopping bricks and kicking ass—I'd been picked on a lot in school.

We studied the art of Shotokan, which mostly deals with self-defense. Shotokan is developed from various martial arts such as judo and aikido, but mostly from karate.

There were three instructors, and they were all very strict. It felt like boot camp. Class would start with stretching, mostly the legs. Then we would do push-ups. Not the standard push-ups where your palms are on the floor. No, we did push-ups on our knuckles!

"Are you kidding me?" I thought. How was I gonna do this on a wooden floor? Because of the CP, my left hand is weaker than my right. The other kids did the exercises like they were nothing, and I felt inferior.

I already worried that I was weak and lazy. Before I started studying Shotokan, I never did any physical exercise. If I got into a fight, it'd be easy to knock me to the ground because I had no balance. We did five sets of 20 exercises, (sit-ups, push-ups, and leg stretches). I had never been so exhausted.

The second week, we got our uniforms and belts. As beginners, we started with white belts. As you get promoted by passing a test, you get different color belts. Above white was yellow; then green; purple; brown; blue; then either red or black to become a master, which takes years of study.

The name for a karate facility is "dojo," so that's what we called the gym, and we called the teacher "sensei." After stretching and exercising, the sensei taught us self-defense techniques. For instance, our fist and forearms raised horizontally in a salute would be an upward block for when the opponent tries to strike the upper body. There were also middle and downward blocks as well as strikes. You use your arms to intercept your opponent's attack.

Compared to sports like MMA (mixed martial arts), Shotokan is more about relaxing the mind and self-control. In MMA, which has become insanely popular, fighters from all over the world combine different martial arts such as judo, muay thai, wrestling, and street fighting. Fighters in MMA regularly sustain serious injuries.

Shotokan allows you to practice techniques against an imaginary opponent and mirror those techniques against an actual opponent. You don't get hurt when you spar with an opponent.

Most of the kids in the class were in special ed, which meant that they had some type of learning or other disability. Most of them mocked the class. The only people who took the class seriously were a kid named Rodney and me. He was already into Shotokan. I befriended Rodney because I saw the way people were treating him when he practiced his moves in the cafeteria: like an outcast. Like me.

Even though Rodney didn't have an obvious physical disability, we were often paired up to practice moves. The fact that I was sparring with someone I knew made it less like an actual fight. It was nice to have someone to train with who didn't make fun of me.

Soon I was doing exercises I never thought I could do, like touching my toes while stretching my legs. It was very exciting to learn martial arts because not only was I getting stronger and improving my balance, I also was taming my anger. I did this by focusing on what I was studying and resisting the urge to retaliate. The philosophy of Shotokan teaches humility, respect, compassion, patience, and an inward and outward calmness. These teachings, combined with learning a new skill, helped me let go of frustration I felt while dealing with my mom or being bullied.

These teachings helped me stand up for myself rather than crying whenever I got beat up. They also helped me learn self-control and anger management.

Combining these ideas with physical movement also boosted my confidence. Strengthening my legs and my body in general helped me believe in myself. The feeling of being able to walk faster and even run (which I hadn't done much because of my CP) inspired me to keep studying. I didn't give up even when I was tired.

I was teased a lot, even by some of the kids that were in the class. A boy named Timothy was jealous of me because I got promoted before he did. He picked on me every chance he got.

One day, while kids in the class were choosing their kumite (sparring) opponents, Timothy stepped up to me, sparring gloves on, and punched me in the face, which is against the rules. Normally, I'd fall to the floor because I had no balance, but practicing Shotokan helped me maintain my stance. I just stood there, grinned, and mouthed to him, "You're not even worth it." I heard one of the girls in the class whisper: "Oh sh-t!" Then the class let out a loud "OHHHHHH!!!" which meant "Fight! Fight! Fight! Fight!"

Timothy went to throw another punch. Instead of responding in violence, I used one of the self-defense tech-

Shotokan teaches humility, respect, compassion, patience, and an inward and outward calmness.

niques from class. I stepped out of the way and grabbed his wrist. I then put my left leg behind his right leg and swept him to the ground, reciting the battle cry we'd learned. The sensei saw everything and instead of punishing us, she called both of us to the middle of the room.

"Kumite stance," she said. Yes! We were about to spar in order to end this rivalry. "Rei!" she yelled for us to begin. As soon as Timothy's eyes met mine, I gave him a kick to the chest that sent him across the floor. I won the match when he forfeited.

Within a year, I got promoted to yellow belt. While study-ing Shotokan, I've competed in a few tournaments where I've sparred against students on the same level as me. I even faced a brown belt once. He was good on his feet, which threw me off balance. The only way I could've bested him was to use my hands.

I landed a few good punches, but I lost points when I threw punches that were ruled "exceeded contact." Ultimately, I lost the match.

*T*hat match helped me learn to use my attacks wisely when sparring and not lose control. I also learned that I didn't have to prove that I was tougher than anyone, because that wouldn't get me anywhere.

After doing Shotokan, I've gotten stronger both physically and mentally. I had gotten fed up with losing control of my anger and getting beat up at school. I hated that I couldn't do anything about it.

Strengthening my legs and my body in general helped me believe in myself.

I initially wanted to study martial arts to defend myself against bullies. Bullying has become a major issue, sometimes causing the victims to take their own lives due to the humiliation and embarrassment they feel. I didn't want to be weak, and I sure as hell wasn't going to kill myself just because some people don't know how to make friends or accept people who are different.

I couldn't physically do all the kicks the same as everyone else because of my CP. You'd think I'd let that stop me, but no. As long as I tried my best, I could succeed and I did. Doing Shotokan has made me more confident and gave me a clearer, more positive state of mind.

Otis later graduated high school and attended college.

Chris Torres

Struggling With a Learning Disability

By Sarah B.

"You know how to spell it," the teacher yelled. "Sound it out! We just went over this. You're not trying!"

I felt my face get hot, and my hands start shaking. I knew how to spell "hat," but it just wouldn't surface. I didn't even want to try. Not now, not in front of the whole class. "They won't want to be my friends," I thought. "Miss Miller hates me."

That was a typical scene at my elementary school. I was only in 1st grade, and already I knew I was stupid. Everybody was working on spelling harder words, like "because" and "orange," and I couldn't even spell "hat."

At home my younger sister Liza was the cute and funny one. My brother Benji was the overachiever, and I was the shy and stupid one. Ben used to tease me about being stupid and my father would grab him and shake him. "Don't ever talk to your sister like that!" he would yell. That was how I knew Ben was telling the truth. Why else would my dad be so mad?

The school told my parents that I had a learning disability and that I was taking up too much of Miss Miller's time. After 1st grade, I changed schools. Now I was going to a different kind of school in New York City. Central Park East was not a school for children with disabilities, it was just one where teachers had more time. My new school didn't stress correct spelling as much as learning how to think and using creativity. In this school there were no grades or tests and you called teachers by their first names, and all the classrooms were set up like a kindergarten class.

I loved my new teacher, Lucy. She was patient and warm and was always giving hugs around. I loved my new school, but I was still stupid. I couldn't keep up with the rest of the class, but I tried my hardest not to let anybody know it. I didn't want any more attention than the other kids were getting.

Being tested is a horrible feeling. It feels like everything you do is giving something away.

And I was smooth. In this new kind of classroom there was lots of independent work. I could sit by myself and pretend to read or write, and nobody would want to interrupt all my hard work. When Lucy came over to see how I was doing, I could fake it really well. I would tell her what the book was about from the cover, or show her a math problem that I had copied off the boy next to me when he wasn't looking.

But soon they caught up with me and that's when the tutors began. First there was Dr. Bloomingthal. She gave me strange exercises to do like copying pictures, or making up a story about a picture. She would show me a shape with lots of sides and then take it away and ask me to draw it from memory. If I got it right I would get an M&M.

All the time she would write things in her notebook. I knew

she wanted to know what was wrong with my head. I knew I was being tested, and I hated it. It is a horrible feeling. It feels like everything you do is giving something away. My mom knew how much I hated going, so sometimes she would take me to the ballet afterwards.

After Dr. Bloomingthal I had another tutor, and then another, and another after that. I had horrible parent-teacher conferences where everybody was nice to me. Sometimes I wished that they would get mad at me. I wanted the reason to be that I was bad, that I wasn't trying. But it seemed that some people were smart, and some were slow, and I was one of the slow ones. I wanted to be smart so badly. There were two boys in my class, Wally and Ronald, who always had the answers. I wanted to be like them.

In 4th grade I was left back. I was relieved, because I was terrified of 5th grade. That year I made friends with a girl named Sara who was a year younger than I was. Sara was the kid who always did the best on spelling tests, and was always asked to give the book reports. Sara was nice, funny, and smart, and right away I was drawn to her. Sara made me want to try hard to do better, and I did. Pretty soon I was learning.

I was still far behind, but things were getting better. My tutors were showing me how to take my time, how not to tackle a problem all at once, but to do it piece by piece. It was almost as though I just had to decide when to start trying hard.

I got through 6th grade and found myself in junior high school. By the 7th grade I was getting good grades and I had almost forgotten that I was not supposed to be as quick as everybody else. That year I asked my principal if I could skip a grade and go back with people my own age. She said yes. I was so happy that I walked around smiling for weeks.

By 10th grade I had learned how to deal with my disability. Now I was normal. I wanted to go to a competitive college and have lots of intellectually stimulating ideas to amaze people with.

Different but Equal

Then the tests started again. I took the PSAT. I knew it would be hard, but this was ridiculous. During the test I got anxious because of the time. The test was asking me to compare different groups of numbers that didn't seem to have anything to do with each other. There were questions where I knew what they were asking but had no idea how to figure it out. Words were popping up, and I had no clue what they meant. I found myself looking around the room, losing my focus. During the break my friends were talking about different questions, but I couldn't even remember them. That test rolled right over me, and left me for dead.

I didn't know what hit me until I got my score. All of a sudden I was stupid again. I got depressed and started to slack off in school. I figured there was no way I could go to college, and now I was scared. My world was falling apart. I let that one test tear away all the confidence that I had spent years building up.

I didn't tell anybody about my scores. It was too humiliating. Then during the summer I decided to tell my boyfriend. Damian didn't pity me; he didn't make me feel like my parents always had. Damian told me not to let these tests get in my way, that if I tried my hardest I could still do well on the SAT. I didn't want to admit it, but something in what he said got through to me. I held on to those words.

In 11th grade I took it again after taking practice tests over and over. I didn't do much better. That was when I sat down to talk to my parents about it. My dad told me honestly that even if I did much better, it would not be good enough for the competitive colleges I wanted to go to, like Brown and Wesleyan. He gave me a list of colleges that don't require SATs but that wasn't what I wanted. I wanted to try. I thought that if I could learn how to spell "hat," I could learn how to do well on this test. My mother had heard that people with learning disabilities could apply to take the test with more time, so that's what I did.

I had to take a test to find out if my learning disability was strong enough to qualify me for extended time. At the end of the 11th grade I was going through the same sort of evaluation that Dr. Bloomingthal gave me all over again. All the same old feelings came back; it was like being in the 2nd grade again. I would start shaking, and cry on the bus home. It was hard.

Finally, after many sessions, the evaluation was over. I was more sad than happy when I found out that I could take the SAT with extended time. I still had a learning disability. They just don't go away.

I'm determined to make this test work for me. So I've been going to Stanley Kaplan, a school that offers classes to help you improve your SAT scores. According to the practice tests

My father gave me a list of colleges that don't require SATs, but that wasn't what I wanted. I wanted to try.

my score has gone up hundreds of points. It hasn't been easy. I've had to work extremely hard but I'm glad I decided to try. Even if those competitive colleges don't take me, after watching that SAT score go up, I feel like I can do anything.

I'm taking the test in two weeks for the last time and I'm scared out of my mind. But whatever happens, I now know that I don't have to let any test take my intelligence away from me. That means much more to me than some number.

Sarah was 17 when she wrote this story.
She later graduated from Oberlin College.

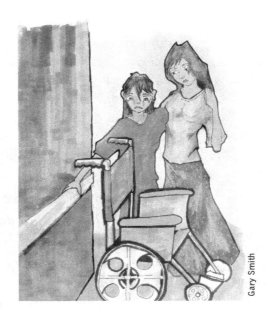

Gary Smith

Facing Reality

By Tania Morales

When I was 13 and living in my native country, Argentina, I realized that I was walking slower than usual and my legs were getting weaker. My mom noticed that my spine wasn't straight. She took me to different doctors, but they didn't know why I had these problems. So she decided we should visit the rest of my family in New York and see an American doctor. (My father, brothers, and sister had moved here a few years earlier.)

I was thrilled about traveling to New York. And when we got there my sister gave us tours around the city. But I kept on holding my mom or sister's hand to stay balanced. And one day after walking around the huge malls of Long Island, I was so tired and my legs hurt very much.

"What's up with my legs now?" I asked myself. I thought of ugly answers like having some kind of cancer and dying, but I couldn't imagine getting sick while I was in the "land of dreams."

Still, I'd also come to New York to go to a doctor. Going to an American hospital was part of my adventure at first. But after about three weeks of seeing many doctors who kept asking for more blood tests, I got bored and frustrated. I wanted them to find the problem, fix it, and let me go.

Then one day I was sitting outside the doctor's office waiting for my sister, while the doctors spoke to her and she translated it to my mom in Spanish. Through the door, I heard my sister and mom sobbing. When they came out they looked very sad, but they didn't say anything.

I felt scared and worried, but I didn't ask why they were crying because if it was bad news, I didn't want to hear it. I was afraid that the truth would be too awful to bear.

Even when my mom and sister took me to physical therapy, I denied that I needed it. I'd tell them, "There is nothing wrong with me," and cut off any conversation that came near the subject of me being sick.

All I knew was that the doctors diagnosed me with "Frederick's ataxia." My family didn't tell me the details, maybe because they could tell I wasn't ready to handle it. What they knew—and I didn't yet—was that it's a genetic disease that makes walking, speech, and control of the hands more and more difficult. There is no cure.

Sometimes I'd think about my life before I came to this country. I had a lot of friends. I'd have bike races with them or play video games with the guys (and I always beat them), or go to the park and just hang around. I loved dancing, and I'd watch music videos and learn all the steps.

But now my walking was getting worse very fast, and I had to hold onto someone everywhere I went because I needed the support. This scared me because I knew what it meant, but I wasn't ready for it. I tried not to think about my sickness, and I was successful at distracting myself, visiting the Statue of Liberty, the Prospect Park Zoo, malls, movies, and restaurants.

Then after six months in the U.S., my brother-in-law brought home a wheelchair, my biggest fear. I was really shocked, and refused to sit in "that thing." I promised to do exercises with my legs and work more on my walking because I just couldn't accept that I had to use the wheelchair, that I wasn't going to be able to go back to my country as I'd left it, walking.

But my family convinced me to use the wheelchair by telling me that if I worked more on my exercises, I wouldn't have to use it. At home I just walked around holding onto the wall or the furniture. There wasn't much room for a wheelchair anyway, and there was no elevator. But when we went out, they took me everywhere in it.

I felt sad and ashamed to be in a wheelchair. I thought everyone was looking at me, so I lowered my head and looked down. I couldn't face the world. I tried to stand up as much as possible because I didn't want people to think I was different. I didn't want to think I was different. And as long as I didn't know about my disease, I could believe that one day, my life would get back to the way it was.

But my life was different. There wasn't any school in my town in Argentina that I could go to in a wheelchair. So when September came, my sister arranged for me to go to 8th grade at MS 2 in Brooklyn, New York, which was wheelchair accessible and near their house.

I couldn't speak English well, and even worse, I was in a wheelchair. But my first day of school turned out great because I was in an ESL class and I didn't need to speak much English. Best of all, my classmates didn't seem to care that I was in a wheelchair. They treated me like a "normal" teen, and that is what I wanted above all.

There were other kids in my school in wheelchairs, but I was the only one in my class and sometimes I felt out of place. It was difficult not to notice the surprised look on some of the kids' faces when I went from class to class. It hurt sometimes and I felt that they thought I was stupid since I couldn't walk.

But my classmates were cheerful, and they made me forget about those looks in no time. They often took me down the hall running or, just before the teacher saw them, hid with me in the elevator. I loved when the other kids took me with them and made me part of their games. I felt like a normal teen.

And I quickly made a best friend, Fior Rodriguez, who's from the Dominican Republic. After two days, we were talking non-stop to each other and soon we got very close.

Fior is like a sister because we know everything that's going on in each other's lives,

Fior treats me like a fellow teen and not like a fragile child.

like what guys we like, what situations make us uncomfortable, and which Spanish music video is our favorite. Fior looks out for me, but her concern about me is different than my family's. Fior treats me like a fellow teen and not like a fragile child.

I made many other friends by the end of 8th grade, and I graduated from junior high with good grades even though I was often absent for doctors' visits. I also left class for physical therapy in the school's gym. It was fun because we'd bowl or play basketball and so it didn't feel like physical therapy at all.

Over the summer, I continued physical therapy at Kings County Hospital three times a week. I'd do a lot of special exercises to make my legs and arms stronger, like ride the bike or sit on a big red ball and try to keep my balance.

My hopes rose because I was able to walk more than I had been. Even though my balance was as bad as ever, I thought that with more therapy, it would improve. I dreamed of starting high school walking like a "normal" teen.

But when I started 9th grade at Brooklyn International High School, I was still in a wheelchair, and now I was the only one in a wheelchair at school. I felt more out of place than I had in junior high.

I could see the other girls walking and staying after school, talking to friends or doing after-school programs. I couldn't stop thinking that before I came to this country, I wanted to have a life like them. "But now I can't because I'm sick, because I can't walk," I'd think. "Why me?"

My disease was developing, and now my handwriting was getting slower. I felt ashamed of not being able to walk or copy notes or do my work fast enough, and sometimes I became shy around other teens. I'd think, "Are they looking at me? Do they think I'm different?"

Sometimes I felt angry or very sad, but I still didn't want to know about my disease. I just couldn't bring myself to think about what my disease was or what would happen to me in the future.

Dealing with the present was tough enough. I couldn't stay after school because it was difficult to get transportation for me. At 3 p.m. I had to wait for the yellow bus to pick me up. I'd go home, do my homework and watch novelas (Spanish soap operas) and American movies. Many times I thought, "I always have to stay inside this box while other teens have fun," wishing I were outside playing, talking to friends, and having a good time.

Now it hit me that I was in a strange country, and I missed my friends from Argentina. Sometimes I just wanted to go back and be with my friends there. We still kept in touch by phone and e-mail. They knew me as the healthy, cheerful, and happy Tania and understood how bad this was for me.

I rarely went outside except for school and church. Every Sunday I got excited because I would go outside, even though it was only to church. I felt good when I was in church because God was and is my biggest support and strength.

Still, sometimes I thought that God was responsible for my inability to walk and I got angry. My family would tell me that I shouldn't blame God for my disease, that God does everything for a reason. I felt annoyed when they told me that because it sounded completely stupid. I'd just sit there playing with my hair, asking myself, "What reason is there to make me stop walking properly if I was just fine the way I was?"

When I slept, I dreamed I was walking and doing so many things, like running with other teens or just being around guys. When I woke up, I felt like my reality was the nightmare.

Fior was always there to listen, talk, and comfort me when I was depressed. Once when I got really sad because I'd had a stupid fight with my mom, I called Fior.

"If I see you crying or sad, it breaks my heart," she said. "You are my strength and you have to be strong." I felt better after that because someone was counting on me to give her strength and I didn't want to let her down. I felt more useful rather than a burden.

On the Internet no one could see me, so they couldn't judge me for not being able to walk properly.

But it was hard to keep from thinking about all the problems my disease was causing, and little by little I stopped doing my therapy. I didn't see why I should continue if it was of no use. I still couldn't walk. I saw everyone living a healthy life, walking, and when someone in my family tried to talk to me, I'd just hide by busying myself with something so they'd go away.

I preferred communicating over the Internet. Since no one could see me, they couldn't judge me for not being able to walk properly. Plus, I didn't have to speak English, only write it, so I didn't have to pronounce hard words.

When I got home from school, I'd go on the computer and stay online for hours. I didn't talk to my family like I used to and that made my mom mad. She also thought I was "doing bad things and talking to maniacs" when I was online. We got into fights over it, which pained me because I didn't like to fight with her.

But sometimes I felt good that she thought I was doing bad things because I know that's what many people think of teens, and it was comforting to know that she thought that I behaved like other teens. It made me feel less different.

At first I went to many different chat rooms with games. My father had taught me how to play dominoes when I was little so I started playing a lot in a dominoes room. I liked being able to practice and talk to people at the same time, especially because I often won. It felt great when they said, "Wow, you are a smart and lucky young lady!"

I made some close friends, though I didn't tell them about me being in a wheelchair. Adam, 17, makes me laugh and his comments show me he knows how to listen. I like that Adam tells me his problems and appreciates my advice. Jason, 19, speaks Spanish and has become like a brother to me.

And Sally, about 38, treats me like a daughter by listening and giving me advice. She even visited me and my family from Texas for a few days last summer. I talked to my dominoes friends every day and I felt that they understood me.

They made me feel more comfortable about myself and I started to feel more tolerant of people who looked at me with curiosity and sadness.

With the breeze hitting my face, I felt free, powerful, and brave.

Wherever I went people often asked me why I was in a wheelchair and I'd just say that I have a disease. But my answer started to seem unsatisfying to me. After three years of not wanting to know about what I had, I realized I was curious, too. Besides, I wasn't getting better and it no longer seemed possible to ignore the disease.

So I did some online research, just to get the basics. I was amazed to see that other teens have Frederick's ataxia because I thought that it was just me. In fact, it's a genetic disease (that means that the disease is in my body's cells) that mostly develops during childhood.

I was really sad when I read that some people with this disease die in early adulthood if heart problems develop. I have some heart problems and that scared me a lot.

I instantly talked to Sally, Adam, and Jason about it because they were the ones I felt closest to at the time. They tried to comfort me. They told me not to think about it because no one knows when we are going to die and that God is the one who decides when we have to go and when we have to stay.

Those words helped me feel a little more confident about living today and not worrying about the future. Since I hadn't told them I had a disease, I was worried that they'd feel disappointed with me and treat me differently. I was relieved to see that nothing changed between us.

But I still felt shocked and sad by what I learned about my disease. It will continue getting worse as I get older. I didn't talk to anyone else about it, not even Fior, because I didn't want them to worry or pity me. I just couldn't stand people feeling sorry for me.

Learning more about Frederick's ataxia freaked me out, but instead of sinking me into more of a depression, it made me get out of my shell and stop feeling sorry for myself. I felt that I have to live all the life I have left, even though it sounded a little stupid because it wasn't like I only had 10 days left. So I tried to get outside and have as much fun as possible.

On a trip to the park with my mom and sister, when we got to the top of a hill, I asked my mom to let go of my wheelchair. She was worried and refused, but I said, "Please Mom! Let me go, please!" until she said yes.

I went down the hill really fast. I smiled triumphantly at people on bicycles as I flew down the hill. With the breeze hitting my face, I felt free, powerful, and brave.

When I reached the bottom of the hill, I had to wait for my mom and sister to come down. It was funny because they looked like they were going to have heart attacks, but after they saw that I was OK they calmed down.

I'd play hide-and-seek with my nephew and niece when we went to stores, too. We'd rush all over the store and try to hide between the rows of clothes. It felt awesome when I played with them. It was as if time stopped for me so I could think and feel that I was part of something. It made me want to have moments like these every day.

Not long ago, I had surgery, not related to my disease, to take a "mass" out of my pituitary gland (a gland that controls hormones). Three days before the surgery, I went to the hospital to fill out some papers and the nurse, Jeffery, saw that I was nervous. He started to talk to me.

Learning more about Frederick's ataxia freaked me out, but it also made me get out of my shell.

I was touched when he said, "I know that you ask yourself, 'Why am I like this and other teens can walk and run and have a good time while I'm in a hospital?' You have to remember that God puts us on this Earth for a reason. Maybe your reason for being like this is because you have to give an example to others that you can do wonderful things even though you are in a wheelchair and you have to face so many problems."

It was exactly what I wanted to hear. Even though it was the same thing that everyone, especially my family, had been telling me, I really listened to Jeffery. I felt that he understood me and that he knew what I was thinking and feeling. And when he looked me in the eyes, I saw that he was telling the truth.

After the surgery I went to the recovery room and for the first time I had the experience of being around other kids under treatment or having surgery. I never thought there were so many small kids with the same or worse problems than me.

It made me feel bad because they were so small and they had so much life—running around, jumping, smiling, and complaining to their doctors because they're always getting pinched with needles. I was older and I didn't have the energy and happiness they did.

I had to stay in the hospital for a week, but my family took turns staying beside my bed day and night, even though they had to eat that nasty hospital food. I saw how much they loved me and I thought how selfish I'd been that I didn't see it earlier.

When I got home from the hospital, I tried to be with my family as often as possible and show them all the love I have for them. I wanted them to know that I care for and love them as much as they do me.

I now know that I have to have more confidence in myself and look at people and at life with my head up. My doctors told me to keep living my life, that I don't have to worry about what other people think of me and that I shouldn't live with the fear of what will happen in the future. I know that there are other people like me in the world, and they just live their regular lives, too.

So I keep busy with things that interest me. I have two internships, at a teen magazine and at the Prospect Park Zoo, plus I go to an after-school program at the American Museum of Natural History where I learn about astronomy. I get around the city on buses and Access-A-Ride (a door-to-door van service).

I realize that if I do nothing, it only makes me see the dark side of things, but if I'm active and busy, I can see the bright side of everything. I'm starting to explore the world. I feel more confident that I can keep going with the support of God and all the people around me.

Tania was 17 when she wrote this story. She later graduated from John Jay College of Criminal Justice in New York City.

David Najarro

Making It in the Real World

By Slade Anderson

During junior high school I went to the New York Institute for Special Education, a school for the blind and visually impaired. It wasn't quite like a regular school. As a blind person I had practically everything I needed: Braille writers, talking computers, Braille books. I was able to run errands for teachers, and help other kids get around school and understand their work.

At one point I even had the option of taking some "mainstream" classes across the street at a regular high school.

But there were many things about the Institute that I didn't like. A lot of the students had other problems besides being visually impaired or totally blind. Some of them were off in their own worlds and used to talk to themselves, laugh out loud, mimic other people or jump up and down and rock back and forth. (These weird habits are sometimes referred to as "blindisms.")

And that wasn't all. Teachers and staff had to follow you around or know exactly where you were at all times. I hated that. I also hated having to get picked up by a school bus at 6:40 every morning. It was an hour and a half each way between my house and the Institute so there was no way I could hang out after school. If I wanted to go around my own neighborhood, I had to go with my father, mother, or sister.

"What kind of teenage life is this?" I thought. I felt like only half a person. I felt cut off from my friends from elementary school. I'd see some of them at the Lighthouse for the Blind on Saturdays. These were kids with little or no vision who were going to public school and taking mainstream classes.

My friend Billy was going to Edward R. Murrow High School. "You should come to Murrow, man. It's cool," he said. He talked about the girls there and the resource room where visually limited kids could go to have their work enlarged, put in Braille, or read out loud to them. Billy was making it in the real world and I wanted that for myself.

Another friend of mine, Mike, told me about the Christmas parties they had. It sounded like if I went to that school I'd have everything I ever wanted: girls, friends, parties, popularity, and people to help me with my print work.

I also found my way around using landmarks like cracks on the floor, pillars, and garbage cans.

One day after going to the Lighthouse I approached my mother about it. I told her I wanted to go to Murrow. I told her Billy went there along with other kids who were totally blind. "I want to broaden my social life," I said. "And my grades are good so I know I can do well in a mainstream class." The next day we took a bus ride just to see how far Murrow was from my house.

After that I arranged a visit. When I got there, there were a million kids in the hallway. I went upstairs and met Mrs. Simon, the resource room teacher, and saw some of my old friends. Mrs.

Simon asked my friend Chris to show me around. I'd never been in such a big school or met so many nice people. "You get around this big school without getting lost?" I asked Chris.

He just laughed and said, "You'll get it down in no time."

In one of the hallways I met a kid named Ricky who was totally blind. He had a guide dog and a lot of girls around him. "Just imagine that being me," I thought.

*I*transferred into Murrow. For the first week or so, my mother brought me to school; then I started taking a school bus. The change from the Institute to Murrow wasn't too drastic because I already knew so many people. Plus there was a resource room where I could get extra help, and I started out taking special education classes.

In the resource room I had people dictate class notes, math problems, or whatever else I couldn't read on my own. The teachers assigned kids to take me from class to class, and if a kid couldn't take me, the teacher or a paraprofessional would do it themselves.

My friend Chris helped me get acclimated to the school. My first year we were in the school production of *The King and I* together. Chris (who has a little vision) helped me get around the stage and interact with the rest of the cast. Chris was very sociable, and knowing there was another person with limited vision getting along with the rest of the kids helped bring me out of my shell. It turned out to be a great experience.

As time progressed I started to take mainstream classes. The first one I remember setting foot into was Spanish. I had taken a little Spanish at the Institute and wanted to see how I'd do so Mrs. Simon asked the teacher to let me sit in on the class. The work moved at a much faster pace than the special ed. classes I was taking. The kids didn't stop the teacher quite as often either. They also behaved a little better.

The teacher gave us a list of new words. She'd say the word and then the whole class would repeat it. I could pretty much follow that. But when she started to give out handouts I really felt isolated. I took the handouts anyway and went over them later with someone in my resource room. A lot of the low-vision kids had to do that or ask one of the kids next to them for help.

While I was working towards becoming mainstreamed, I also took "mobility training." We made a tactual map (a raised map you can feel with your fingertips) of the school and I learned how the hallways and classrooms were set up numerically. I also found my way around using landmarks I could feel, like cracks on the floor, pillars, and garbage cans.

I worked on the bus trip to and from the school with Cindy, my mobility teacher. We practiced getting to the bus stop, then taking the bus home, and after that on the trip to school. It took a lot of work but on the morning that she told me I was finally "cleared" to travel by myself it was almost like getting a license to drive. That's how free I felt. It was a big accomplishment.

But mainstreaming isn't something that happens overnight and then you're done. You have to work at it. The bus I had to take didn't run very often and sometimes it would rush right past me without stopping. After a while I made friends with some of the drivers, though, and they would know to stop for me. One driver knew me so well that when I wasn't on his bus in the morning the next day he'd ask me, "Playing hooky again, huh?"

Going into a mainstream program was scary, but life at the Institute for the Blind was too sheltered.

Even after I worked my way out of special ed. and was taking regular classes with sighted kids, I still had obstacles to overcome. During one cycle I had gym class on the 4th floor. To get there you had to go through two different gyms and up a flight of stairs. After I changed out of my gym clothes I never had enough time to get to math class. The teacher told me he didn't mind my being late but I felt uncomfortable about it. It made me appear disabled.

Without consulting my resource room teacher I went straight

to my guidance counselor and requested a schedule change. When Mrs. Simon heard about it she was upset. She felt I was going over her head—and getting in over mine. She said the class I had requested had a teacher who once had a bad experience with a blind student and she was concerned about that. I took the class anyway and got an "excellent."

With every success story there is a little hardship, however. People still shy away from me because I'm visually impaired. Sometimes instead of saying "Hi, Slade" they say, "Watch that stick." Others feel embarrassed if I ask them to read something to me softly.

Going into a mainstream program was a big and scary decision but I'm still glad I made it. Life at the Institute was too sheltered. At Murrow I learned that I can't always have a Braille book handed to me at the same time the print users get theirs. I learned that there is life outside the blind world and if I want to be a part of it, I have to go out and take some risks.

Slade was 18 when he wrote this story. He attended SUNY Oneonta, Hunter College, and the Colorado School for the Blind.

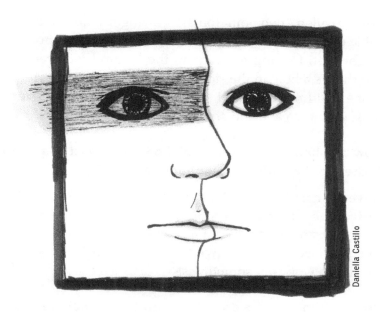

Daniella Castillo

What's It Like Being Blind?

By Slade Anderson

These are some of the questions sighted people have asked me about being blind (and some that people would probably like to ask me if they weren't too embarrassed).

Q: Do you know what you look like? If so, how? Did somebody tell you?

A: I know what I look like by the use of touch. I've also been told what color my hair and eyes are and had a sighted person measure my height and my weight.

Q: How do you get around and how do you know where you're going?

A: I get around using a cane to feel what's in front of me. I use a technique called "two point touch." I swing my cane to the opposite side of my body than my foot is landing. If I'm stepping with my right foot, I swing my cane to the left and vice versa. That way if there's a hole in the sidewalk coming up on the right side my cane will find it before I step with the right foot. I'll feel the dropoff with my cane and step back.

Q: How do blind people have fun? Do they only sit in a room and listen to the radio or audiobooks all day?

A: I love watching movies. I listen to what's going on and take an educated guess about what's on the screen. If I have no idea at all I ask whomever I'm with. I also like to go to the beach in the summer and ice skate in the winter. I like singing and listening to music. I also work out sometimes.

Q: How do blind people dress themselves? Do their parents have to dress them? How do they know what they're wearing?

A: I usually ask someone if what I've picked out matches. Some blind people have other systems of doing it like labeling their clothes. They label them in larger print or even in Braille by color.

I fold all my bills differently. I fold my $20 bills like a triangle and my $10 bills like a square.

Q: How do blind people read and write? Do they learn by just listening?

A: I read Braille. That's a system of raised dots on a page that you can feel with your fingertips. Different dot combinations mean different things. I write with a Braillewriter, which has six keys and a space bar. I also have a little machine that lets me hear what I'm writing and also prints it out in Braille and regular print. To write, you press different key combinations for different letters.

Q: How do you go to the bathroom and wash yourself?

A: I go to the bathroom like everybody else. If I'm in a public place I ask where it is and naturally I know where it is in my own house. I walk up to the toilet until my shins hit the edge and then move back a couple steps. That way I don't miss. As for hygiene, I wash myself, dress myself, cut my own nails, brush my own teeth, shave myself, comb my own hair, etc.

Q: How do blind people deal with money? Do they just carry one dollar bills around or how does that work?

A: I have a system where I fold all my bills differently. I fold my $20 bills like a triangle and my $10 bills like a square.

Q: How do blind people sign their names? Do they just put an "X"?

A: Blind people learn to sign their names like everyone else.

The only difference is that some learn later in life and use something called a signature guide. That's a metal or cardboard rectangle with a window in the middle of it. A sighted person places the window over the place on the page where you're supposed to sign.

Slade was 18 when he wrote this story.

Stuttering Controlled My Life

By Joanna Fu

It's back in 7th grade, the day I have to give my oral presentation on pandas. I've been thinking about this day for three months—ever since my science teacher first announced that, in addition to a term paper, she was also making us do an oral presentation. Most people hate speaking in front of a crowd, but for me it is especially torturous because I stutter.

I don't want to humiliate myself, so I have practiced my presentation over and over again—in front of the mirror, and for audiences of my parents and siblings, my grandparents, and my friends. I brushed my teeth three times this morning and I'm wearing my silver cross necklace and special blue striped shirt, all to give me luck.

As I walk into class and sit down, I can feel my palms getting sweaty and I can hear my breath echoing in my ears. Trudging up the aisle to the waiting podium, I make a fervent plea for some kind of divine intervention. (None comes.)

I make a show of organizing my already organized papers and fiddling with my posterboard. As I shuffle the cards around, I can see my hands trembling, feel my stomach churning, and taste the bile rising in my throat.

Finally, I gather up enough courage to speak. The class settles to a hush and I can see 24 pairs of eyes looking expectantly at me. I open my mouth to speak. Nothing comes out.

I try to speak again, but still nothing comes out. This is called a stuttering block. It feels like something is stuck in my throat, making it impossible for any sounds to come out. This usually happens when I'm under a lot of pressure or when I'm speaking in front of a big group of people—like now.

I look up and see 24 increasingly annoyed faces. I try to spit out my words this time, only to end up stuttering: "M-m-m-m-y s-s-s-s-scie-e-e-ence fair p-p-project i-is about p-p-pandas."

I can hear a slow titter run throughout the class, as people exchange looks that scream, "Did you hear that? Did you hear her try to talk? Wasn't that hilarious?"

I see 24 pairs of eyes looking expectantly at me. I open my mouth to speak. Nothing comes out.

I blush and continue to stumble through the rest of the presentation. When I am finally done, I slink back to my seat as Dr. Klein pityingly says, "Nice try, Joanna, nice try."

That was just one of many times when I was totally humiliated because of my stuttering. I don't remember exactly when it started, but it was a problem through most of my childhood.

From about 3rd grade on, my stuttering basically controlled my life. I never really knew which words or letters I would start stuttering on, so everything I said was a potential bomb.

When I would stutter was more predictable—it usually cropped up during stressful situations, like when teachers called on me to answer a question or when I was doing a skit in drama class.

Or when I had to say my name, since I was expected to reply immediately, without any time to stall or to prepare. You see, I would usually stall to avoid saying words I knew would make me stutter. I'd say things like, "What's that word again? It's a really big animal in Africa...it's like...it starts with an e..." and hope that the person I was talking to would provide the word so I would not have to say it.

*I*t's hard to do that with your own name. Believe me, I've tried. I remember one time in elementary school, I was trying out for my school's chorus and had to say my name to sign up.

I had a silver bracelet with my name engraved on it, and I thought I could just hold it up for the music teacher to see. But I ended up sitting too far away for the teacher to be able to read it. So I spelled my name to avoid actually saying it.

A more typical scene goes like this:

"Hi, what's your name?"

"My name is...My name is...is..."

(Laughter) "What's the matter? Forgot your own name?!"

Stuttering wasn't just a problem at school. I even stuttered at home around my parents and siblings. And they teased me as much as strangers did.

My family's derision hurt even more because I expected them to support me, not laugh at my problem. Even worse, I usually couldn't even respond to their taunts because I knew I would start stuttering under the stress of talking back.

I often felt alienated from my family and I grew apart from them, mainly because my stuttering and their reaction to it made it hard for me to talk to them. My parents never really said anything about my stuttering to me. I think that they thought it was like an itchy mosquito bite—something temporary that, if you just ignored it, would go away in its own time. Or they acted like it was something I did on purpose to get attention.

At one point, my mother started forcing me to pick up the phone and call restaurants and travel agencies to make reservations, knowing that these were extremely stressful situations for me and that I wouldn't be able to speak. She thought that if I did this enough times, it would break me out of my "bad habit" of stuttering.

My sister and brother would often listen in on these phone calls, and I could hear howls of laughter when I finally hung up the phone, frustrated and embarrassed.

I was most self-conscious about my stuttering during 7th grade because I was starting all over in a new school and had no friends to depend on—I had to make new ones.

I was between a rock and a hard place when I met new people. I knew that if I spoke extensively to strangers, I would start stuttering. On the other hand, if I responded with only yes or no answers, potential friends would think that I was unfriendly. I never wanted to tell people directly that I stuttered because I was ashamed of being different and "defective," as my sister so kindly put it.

Finally, in the middle of 7th grade, I managed to persuade my mom to bring me to a speech pathologist. (My mom had finally come to the realization that my stutter was a real problem and not something that I made up just for attention.)

I became determined to confront my fear and to get rid of my stuttering. So I joined the school debate team.

I went to see Dr. Nancy once a week for about a year and a half. She just had me talk about anything to get me relaxed and comfortable. Then, every time I stuttered, she would raise her hand and I would go back and try to correct that phrase or sentence.

She would also have me read aloud from newspaper articles and would have me come to group sessions where I would talk with other stutterers. Once, she even went to a fast food place with me and had me order, to help me overcome my stuttering when talking to strangers. During that time, I noticed that while my speech did improve a lot, it still wasn't perfect.

Finally, in 9th grade, I became determined to confront my fear and to completely get rid of all the traces of my stuttering. So I joined the school debate team. Both my brother and sister had been on their school's debate team, and they told me how much fun it was.

There were no tryouts; anybody could join. Debate put a lot of stress on me and, at times, I stuttered more than I had before.

However, I slowly overcame my fear of speaking and became more sure of my own voice. Sometimes, during a round, my speech would be flawless. And I was stuttering less in general, not just when I was debating.

I've changed a lot since that awful 7th grade presentation on pandas. As a senior in high school, I now feel comfortable talking to strangers, calling agencies for information, and leading discussion groups.

I even have a different attitude now—I'm more likely to speak up without having to be asked, or to approach new people and start conversations.

Thanks to my work with Dr. Nancy and on the debate team, I feel that I can now honestly call myself someone who has overcome stuttering. And although at times I may still pause or hesitate to say certain things, I am able to enunciate those magical words, "Hi, my name is Joanna."

Joanna was 15 when she wrote this story.
She later attended Bryn Mawr College,
where she majored in German and art history.

Lee Samuel

My Sister's Keeper

By Anonymous

Many people wonder what it's like to be a twin. Do twins think the same thoughts? Do they share the same feelings? I am a twin, but growing up I never experienced those close connections. My twin sister Nicole (not her real name) is mentally retarded. Her condition put a barrier between us from the beginning.

As we grew up, I started doing things for myself, but she didn't. She couldn't pick out her own clothing or even eat so that food went into her mouth and not anywhere else. My mom was her eyes and hands.

All the attention Nicole got from my mother made me feel competitive. I fought for my mom's attention. I won soccer and hockey games, and the medals mounted up across our room. I did well in math and science, too. But it seemed all the games I won and all my academic awards meant little to my mom.

Whatever pride she showed lasted a brief moment, and then her attention shifted back to Nicole. I felt ashamed to envy someone helpless, but I did.

At the same time, I felt guilty that I had escaped Nicole's fate. What happened to her could have happened to me. Both of us were partly strangled by our umbilical cords in my mother's womb. As we were being born, we were both losing oxygen. I got out first, delaying my sister from coming out. Those last minutes permanently damaged the left hemisphere of her brain. I know it's not my fault, but I still feel guilty—especially because deep down, I can't help feeling glad to be the one who was born unharmed.

I still feel guilty because, deep down, I'm glad to be the twin who was born unharmed.

Until we started our second year of school, Nicole could mostly fit in with the other kids. But as the year progressed, our classmates started to make fun of her. She started to cry over going to school—before she'd been excited to go. Ironically, it made me want to spend more time at school to get away from the hurt she let out at home.

When we reached 3rd grade, my father took the money he'd been saving to buy us a house and instead used it to send me to an expensive private school. Our family of four lived in a one-bedroom apartment, so we could afford tuition. Meanwhile, my sister was stuck in a poorly funded public school. I didn't feel I deserved this lopsided love from my dad and it made me feel ridiculous. My envy turned to shame.

I also began noticing the way my father and his family mistreated Nicole. My father's family used to call Nicole names, which drove my mother to lash out at them and caused problems between her and my father. Meanwhile, Nicole tried hard to get my father's attention, but he ignored her or acted like he was ashamed of her. If she said "Hi" to him, she'd get no reply in return. He'd yell at her when she unintentionally broke stuff in the house, or when she didn't do things as quickly as someone else might. His words still echo in my mind: "What did I do to deserve this?" and, "You're retarded in the mind, not body, so stop embarrassing me!" I was too young and scared to tell my father off, but I wanted to.

By the time I got to junior high, I saw how my sister endured all those heartbreaking comments without standing up for herself, and I began to get angry. I decided my father's actions were making my sister more introverted and delaying her emotional development. I also started to have dreams about my sister. In my dreams she was pitiful and helpless. It was weird, but these dreams woke me up to the bad treatment my sister got in reality. I finally got the message: Nicole needed me.

I decided it was time to stand by her, and I developed a powerful protectiveness toward her. I started thinking, "Why should my sister be the only one who is being looked at as a failure?" I began rebelling in every way I could. My dad wanted me to continue being the champion in sports, so I quit them altogether. He wanted me to play nice with his family; I stopped visiting them. That started a separation between my father and me that still exists.

Meanwhile, Nicole and I were about to become closer. One day, she left behind a science project that she'd worked hard to finish, and I decided it was worth being late to my school to take it to her. It was the first time I'd set foot in her school. It seemed normal, until I was directed to the special education floor. Going through those halls made me want to cry. I saw kids with all kinds of physical and mental disabilities, and all I could think about was their families and the pain they must have gone through. As the crowd thinned, I saw two girls kicking a helpless girl on the floor. The victim was Nicole.

I dropped everything I was holding and slammed one of the girls to the wall. I punched her with all the potency I had. Then someone jumped in and knocked the second bully unconscious. I was charged with assault and disorderly conduct, but the charges were dropped because I was defending my sister. The other girls were expelled. To this day, the thought of the pain they inflicted on my sister makes me feel the anger all over again.

It took this event to make me care about Nicole the way I always should have. After it happened, she finally opened up to me about everything that was going on with her in school and life. She told me how girls wrote hurtful comments about her in the bathroom (thinking she couldn't read it), how boys gave her a hard time, and so much more.

As time went on, I gradually left my friends behind to be there for my sister. I didn't notice until one of them pointed it out. I was accompanying her everywhere she went like she was a baby because I was scared for her safety. But my other reason for pulling away from my friends was remembering how cruel they'd been to the disabled students in our school. They used to shove them to the floor and throw food into their faces. Watching them, I'd tried to suppress images of my sister, and the pain lingered for days. Now the thought of it all just disgusted me.

My worry and stress about what would become of Nicole each day started to give me panic attacks. My heart would start racing and I'd have trouble breathing. My emotional instability was taking a toll on my physical health, but I couldn't stop worrying about my sister.

Then, one day, I watched the movie *The Karate Kid* and got an idea: I would send my sister to Tae Kwon Do and self-defense lessons. I knew it was ridiculous to expect her to be some kind of ninja like in the movies, but just the idea that she could build some self-esteem and develop strength to protect herself made me hopeful. I decided to pay for the self-defense lessons from my birthday and babysitting money.

For the first few days of classes she didn't want me to come.

She said I would make her nervous. I was nervous, too. I was worried she might not understand what was going on in class, and that she wouldn't be accepted. I also did not want to make things worse for her. If her teachers gave up on her, it could deepen the shame she felt about herself.

But seeing her come back from class each day with a less gloomy face soon eased my fears. During the third week, I saw bruises on her arm and part of me wanted to explode. Then I realized it was a relief that, unlike coaches who had rejected her in the past, the people at the Tae Kwon Do school actually treated her as roughly as they treated anyone else. It showed me they had respect for her. They weren't treating her like fragile glass—or like she was nothing.

At the Tae Kwon Do school, they didn't treat my sister like fragile glass—or like she was nothing.

My worries for her self-esteem gradually faded. She started ignoring the nasty stares of girls at school. She seemed less embarrassed and lifted her face more. With her hair tied back for Tae Kwon Do practice, you could clearly see her angelic features.

Since then I've also helped Nicole progress at school by researching where to get affordable extra help for her. I found some amazing state-funded programs that offer free assistance. My mother and I agreed to send Nicole to an educational center that used tutoring, peer group work, and other teaching methods to reach out to disabled students. After a couple of years of hard work, she finally switched some of her special education classes to regular classes.

These days, I'm less anxious about my sister. Last summer in Pennsylvania, she fought her first Tae Kwon Do tournament and won 4th place. As the months have gone on, I've seen beauty in her that I never saw before, all because of this simple sport. She thanks me, but the only credit I take is for putting her in those classes and paying for it. The rest was up to her.

I'm overjoyed at what she's accomplished. But what keeps me up at night is the thought that hatred in this world will never stop and what she's gone through so far may be just the prelude to her future. I'm not sure I'll ever be able to stop worrying. Still, I know that what will also endure is our love for each other. I've learned that love can deepen so much with time, even love for people you've spent your whole life with.

The author was 16 when she wrote this story.

Chris Pope

Deaf but Not Dumb

By Oni Nicolarakis

For 11 years I went to the Lexington School for the Deaf, but when I was 14 I decided I wanted to leave and go to a main-stream school. My biggest fear was that no one would ever be able to understand me when I talked and that I wouldn't be able to understand anyone either.

At Lexington, I felt safe and secure. I had a lot of friends and I'd known my teachers since pre-school. I knew sign language so it was easy for me to communicate with the other deaf students.

But I also began to feel controlled and dependent, and I felt isolated from the hearing world. Though I am the only deaf per-son in my family, I didn't have that many hearing friends, and I wanted some. And I knew I needed to get better at speaking and reading lips in order to communicate with hearing people.

The fact is that in this world, hearing people are in the majority. I knew that in the future I would have to adapt to a hearing world, and I was afraid that the longer I stayed at Lexington, the harder it would be for me to learn to speak and read lips well and to survive on my own. I was also afraid it would make it more difficult for me to get into a good college.

Still, leaving wasn't an easy decision to make. A lot of deaf people tend to want to hang out only with other deaf people, and sometimes they feel that hearing people think they are not just deaf but "deaf and dumb." I'd also had some bad experiences with hearing people in the past. When I was 10, for instance, my best friend (who is hearing) and I went to a candy store in my old neighborhood. I wanted to buy the candy lipstick, but the old man behind the counter didn't understand me and kept saying "What? We don't have peanuts." Because I am deaf, I speak with an accent and sometimes people have trouble understanding me.

I wanted to be mainstreamed, not isolated.

I kept repeating that I wanted the candy lipstick, but he just kept saying that he didn't have any peanuts, again and again. I got really mad when he started taunting me, making fun of my speech. My friend told me that after I left he laughed and told other people that I was stupid. I've had other experiences, too, when I've been unable to understand people or they haven't understood me. But I still wanted to go to a mainstream school.

I got the idea from a friend who had left Lexington several years earlier because she wanted a better education than she felt she was getting. I felt that way too, but I didn't do anything until two years later when I was in the 8th grade. Then I asked my mom if I could go to a hearing high school.

She didn't want me to go. She liked the close environment at Lexington where she knew all of my teachers and friends. She also feared that I wouldn't have any friends at a mainstream school and that students would make fun of me. She told me to think about it for a while before I made my decision. She didn't want me to make a mistake.

I thought about it for a couple of months, both about what I would gain and what I would lose. I was afraid of losing all of my old friends and of not being able to make any new ones.

But I believed that if I stayed at Lexington I wouldn't get the opportunity to get into a good college, and that this would hold me back in life. In the end, I decided I wanted to go, and my mother agreed. I went to my guidance counselor and she helped me identify high schools with resources for deaf students.

I visited two. At the first one, Martin Van Buren HS, all of the students who had hearing loss stayed in one classroom all day long with a teacher who knew sign language. I wanted to be mainstreamed, not isolated.

So I visited the second school, Middle College HS, and I liked what I saw. Deaf students were in the same classes with hearing students, and I decided that's where I'd go.

The first day, I was adamant that I wanted to be independent. I wanted to prove to others that I was capable of taking care of myself. I didn't want anyone to think that I was helpless or an invalid just because I'm deaf. I wanted to be the kind of person who could help others.

But when I walked through the doors of my new school, I felt scared. The first thing I saw were lots of students scrambling around the hallways. I couldn't find the room I was supposed to be in and I didn't want to ask anyone for help. I was afraid that people would ask me to repeat myself over and over or give me special treatment like taking me to my classroom instead of pointing the way.

So I started looking for the classroom myself. I noticed that I was the only one who didn't know anyone in the school. Everyone seemed to know everyone else, and I saw a lot of students kissing each other on the cheek or hugging. No one noticed me.

For 25 minutes I walked in circles trying to find the room. I went into three wrong classrooms and had to say "Oops, I'm sorry," each time. During those 25 minutes I felt scared that I might never find the room. But finally I did.

That was the first challenge I overcame at Middle College HS, but there have been others. For one thing, after that first day, I was given an interpreter who accompanied me in my new school. She translated what the teacher said into sign language, and helped me communicate with people one on one when I had trouble on my own. I felt annoyed when people talked to her instead of to me directly, as if I couldn't read lips at all. But for the most part, she helped a lot.

Even with her there, at first I was shy and I didn't talk to that many people. It seemed like people were afraid to talk to me too because I was deaf.

After a while, though, I started to make more friends. Most of my friends were from American Sign Language class. Some hearing students take it as a foreign language, just like Spanish. In the class I shared my experiences as a deaf teenager. I explained that I like to do a lot of the same stuff other teenagers like to do, like watch movies and videos, shop, and hang out.

Because they knew about me and my culture, my classmates didn't treat me like I was strange.

They learned how to talk to me the way I want to be talked to, face to face, slowly and clearly, and I felt more confident making friends with them. Because they knew about me and my culture, they didn't treat me like I was strange.

Now I have a lot of hearing friends at school, but sometimes I still get frustrated. When my friends talk too fast or all at the same time, for example, I don't always understand them. Occasionally I ask them to repeat what they've said and they say, "Never mind."

When someone tells a joke I didn't understand and everyone starts laughing, sometimes I just laugh along with them, pretending I know what they're laughing about. I don't want to be a bother and ask them to repeat it. But I'd rather know the joke than just pretend.

Going to Middle College HS has changed a lot for me. I have lost the close connections I had with my friends from Lexington. Now instead of seeing them every day, I only get to see them a few times a year. And I don't get to sign that much like I used to. At Lexington, signing was a language we all shared.

But I've gained the experience of making new friends, writing for the school newspaper, and choosing my own classes. I wanted to be more independent, and when I think of this, I

When people look at me and are surprised that I am so capable, I feel that I've succeeded.

feel good about myself and my decision to switch schools. When people look at me and are surprised that I am so capable, I feel that I've succeeded.

After my year at Middle College HS, I felt confident enough to join the teen writing staff at Youth Communication, and take part in the meetings and discussions without the help of an interpreter.

At first, because I was on my own, I was scared to speak out during meetings. Lots of times I didn't understand everything that people said, and I worried that by the time I got my chance to speak, they would have changed the topic and my comment would seem out of place.

But later on I became more assertive and involved. I didn't care so much if what I said was stupid or if I said it at the wrong time. I just wanted to get it over with and say what I had to say.

I know I've grown stronger from my experiences in Middle College HS and in the hearing world. Before, when people didn't accept me because I was deaf, I would feel like I wasn't good enough or that there was something wrong with me. When someone made fun of me, it hurt like I had been punched in the stomach.

But there were so many new challenges and struggles at Middle College HS, being surrounded by hearing people all the time, that I couldn't let myself get down. At first I would think, "Maybe I can't." But then I would tell myself, "I'm beautiful, I'm smart, I'm capable," over and over again, until finally I could believe it.

In the past I was afraid of going off to college with a lot of hearing people and of choosing a career where I would have to work with hearing people. Now I'm more afraid of whether I'll be able to pay for college or if I'll know what career to choose.

My experiences at Middle College HS have made me more confident about myself and more willing to speak out among hearing people and get involved. Maybe the most important thing it's helped me learn, though, is not to be afraid of being independent.

Oni went on to Gallaudet University.
She also served on the board of Deaf Women United.

Ruda Tillett

No Such Thing As Normal

By Fabio Botarelli

If there's any word that deserves to be tossed out of the English dictionary, it's the word "normal." It defines a person in a narrow way and limits creativity. Even worse than "normal" is "abnormal." I should know. I have a learning disability, and I've been labeled abnormal.

I was first diagnosed in kindergarten with a learning disability known as speech and language processing delay. That meant I often had a hard time understanding what people were saying. Sometimes I'd need people to repeat themselves or I'd have to repeat their words myself.

Expressing myself verbally was even more difficult. Whenever someone spoke, I'd take a while to understand the message. When I spoke, it took time for people to understand me.

I misunderstood people and people misunderstood me. My disability was a challenge, but being called abnormal by other children was devastating. It made me feel like I was part of a species that was unfit and should be left to die. At least once a week someone at school called me abnormal, and each time I felt a stake driven deeper into my heart.

Because my mom is French, I attended a French school, Lycee Francais of New York, starting in preschool. Speaking French at school wasn't a problem because my mom spoke French at home.

But other school assignments were difficult. I had trouble comprehending the main idea of a story. I also had a hard time with numbers. Many times my parents had to repeat their instructions slowly and carefully because they sensed that I had trouble understanding what they said. Trying to teach me to play baseball, for example, my father had to physically place my hands on the right part of the bat and position me a certain way because I just didn't understand his directions.

My parents were always there to give me hugs and encouragement, but I never told them I was having trouble with the kids at school.

Feeling frustrated, I'd dream of a world where I was king and my family and I lived in a palace in the clouds, with a never-ending abundance of fun. In that world I had the power to solve any problem and do my homework in 10 seconds. In my fantasy world, every day was a new day to wake up to with countless friends standing over my bed to wish me good morning.

But reality whispered in my ear that I was stupid and slow. In my real life at Lycee, I had very few friends and many enemies — immature brats who devoted their efforts to making my life miserable and making fun of my poor academics.

My parents were always there to give me hugs and encouragement, but I never told them I was having trouble with the kids at school. I was very shy and kept lots of secrets. I was also too proud to tell them about my problems and figured that I could clean up my own mess.

As a result, a lot of ugly emotions built up within me and

transformed from confusion and anguish to anger and hatred. Sometimes when I came home, my parents asked me, "How was your day?" Usually I said, "OK," or "I'm not in the mood to talk." Sometimes I shared a few details, but I never told them too much.

I asked myself what I could never ask them: "Why am I so different? Why can't words come out of my mouth naturally? And why do I say things that other kids laugh at or use to insult me?" It seemed that no one could understand my pain. I felt like a little boy locked behind a closed door, screaming to be rescued.

It wasn't just that I had trouble learning new things. I also had a terrible temper that I couldn't control. Having trouble expressing myself, I resorted to pushing and punching other students.

As far as I was concerned, my peers were making communicating more difficult than necessary and all I was doing was defending my dignity to get the respect that I deserved. Force was always simple and intelligible. What followed was about five trips a month to the principal's office, where I was seated next to my victim and told softly to apologize.

One time, I was playing with my teddy bear snacks in the lunchroom and one of the biggest mouths in my kindergarten class asked why I was so weird.

"Leave me alone, I'm eating," I said.

"You're just a sissy who everyone hates," he said, throwing my bag of teddy bear cookies on the floor and stepping on them. That was more than enough oil to start my fire. I got up from my table, charged at him and landed a punch on his jaw. He started bleeding and crying hysterically, but I was in such a blind rage that I stuffed him like a turkey, remembering all the times he and his friends had picked on me. Most of my punches were aimed at his mouth, which in my mind represented an instrument of oppression.

Not surprisingly, I was almost expelled, which made me feel that everyone was against me and that only my family could provide me with shelter. My parents weren't too happy to hear that their son was a Rocky in the making, but they also understood my pain. They cautioned me to keep my hands to myself.

Their advice didn't work. By the end of kindergarten, the principal—after handing them a list of all the kids I'd hit and discussing my disability in language processing—asked my parents to send me to another school.

So my parents decided to transfer me to Parkside, a new private school in Manhattan for kids with learning disabilities, for 1st grade. I approved of their decision because I always had this illusion that the future would be better. That was one good thing about being 5. I was too ignorant to understand what was happening.

I still had trouble expressing myself, but my new classmates and teachers understood how I felt and guided me.

My parents knew that Parkside was the right school for me, because it possessed a nurturing environment, small classrooms, and best of all, other kids with learning disabilities and poor social skills. It didn't take me long to blend in. In the first week of 1st grade, I made seven friends. Having many friends made me feel good about myself. Now home wasn't the only place I felt wanted.

In the weeks that followed, my parents were finally able to breathe. I still had trouble expressing myself, but my new classmates and teachers understood how I felt and guided me, reminding me to pay attention and use words to defend myself. Eventually such methods became routine for me. As for the course work, I had a little trouble at first with the directions. My teachers helped me by giving me hints before I took my homework home and told me to pay close attention to the first sentence of every paragraph.

My mom still had to force me to do my homework. Sometimes she waited with me as late as 11 p.m. until I finally gave in and started my homework. Once or twice I had the feeling that she was ready to strangle me for my stubbornness. But her hard work paid off. By 4th grade, I was demanding extra work from my teachers. I was now in the most advanced math class and the work was still easy. My parents could see how much their son, once a small and troubled youngster, had improved.

At that time, I still didn't know that I had a learning disability. During all those years at Parkside, I actually believed that I went to a regular school. I had loving parents, understanding teachers, and wonderful friends with whom I could share laughs. Every child at my school had his or her own set of problems, and I considered that normal. Some of my friends were outrageous individuals with their heads in the clouds, but they were normal to me.

I found out I had a learning disability because of my academic success at Parkside. My father decided to transfer me to Churchill, a more academically challenging school for kids with learning disabilities in Manhattan, instead of letting me graduate from Parkside in 5th grade.

I asked him why. Leaving meant abandoning my friends, people I had grown up with for years. He told me that Parkside was no longer challenging enough for me.

He told me that I was born with a disability which makes it difficult for me to learn, but has nothing to do with how smart I am. After his explanation, I understood and felt relieved. I realized that I had come a long way and for that I was happy.

But leaving my friends after four years was heartbreaking. It was so hard to leave everything behind. Angel and Kevin, two of my good friends, were also leaving. Although we were transferring to new schools for 5th grade, Parkside generously included us in the 5th grade graduation ceremony. At graduation, the three of us lined up in front of a microphone to sing "I Believe I Can Fly."

This song was a spiritual portrait of dreams come true and as I stood in the back of the trio while Angel and Kevin were croaking out the lyrics, I wondered if I should say goodbye too. Breaking ahead of the two, who were by then groaning like grumpy old men, I hoisted the microphone from its place and erupted into melodious song. Angel and Kevin gathered around me on each side and we sang the last two minutes of the song.

Parents erupted in tears, my principal had to go to the bathroom to get a tissue and the three of us bumped stomachs in mid-air. We felt like the Three Musketeers that day. But more importantly, we'd given our parents confidence that we were changing already. The future was a whole bunch of new chapters to look forward to in our lives.

Today I'm a senior at Churchill School. I still struggle in large settings, but I thrive in small groups. Kids at school know me for what I can do. For instance, I have a passion for writing and running. I'm a nationally ranked chess player and I've won many accolades in tournaments in and outside of school.

I've refused to let my learning disability hold me back from becoming what I want to be. Instead of letting emotions build up inside me, I vent them in a positive way and keep myself busy.

I'm a little nervous about college because I've been in special education almost my entire life. A mainstream environment is going to be a culture shock, but I'm ready for it. I won the battle over my disability years ago when it was at its most severe stage.

I want people who have learning disabilities to know they should push beyond what society expects of them. There are no limits. The universe has no end. As for you "regular" kids, I want you to know that there is no such thing as normal. To label different people as abnormal not only limits our understanding of human nature but also deprives us of the ability to see the beauty in each of us.

Fabio was 18 when he wrote this story. After high school,
he attended Trinity College in Connecticut.

Gamal Jones

Getting the Words Out

By Gamal Jones

A little while back, my oldest brother Deron bought a fighting fish that he named Philippe (he pronounced it Fill-lee-pay). We were hanging out at our mom's house with our other brother, Michael, talking about the fish as it swam around its bowl on the kitchen counter.

"What if it's a girl, and I'm naming it Philippe?" Deron joked.

I countered, "Since you're unsure of the gender, you should name it Sh-sh-she-"

Deron giggled as he finished my statement, "I should name it She-llipe?!"

Although I'd made my brothers laugh, I was frustrated that I'd stuttered and hadn't communicated the joke flawlessly like I wanted to.

I'm 20 years old now, and I've stuttered since I was 5.

Sometimes I get stuck on a word and other people fill in the gaps for me, like with my brothers and the fish. Other times, I'll choose another word because I can't get my first choice out. Or I'll say something like "um," or pretend I'm trying to remember what to say to buy time—so what I say doesn't come out in a stutter.

I know I'm going to stutter on a word before I even say it, and I feel so frustrated and angry when it happens. I sound like a skipping CD, with my words getting repeated and chopped up. I get sick and tired of my messages not coming out the way I intended. I want to have clear speech.

> *I know I'm going to stutter on a word before I even say it, and I feel so frustrated and angry when it happens.*

My earliest memory of someone laughing at me because of my stutter was in 4th grade. I was giving a presentation in front of the class, stuttering here and there, when I heard low-toned snickering coming from a classmate.

When it was his turn to go up, my teacher, in an exaggerated fashion, pretended to laugh at him while he was giving his presentation—just like he'd done to me. He began to cry, and then she delivered a "Do unto others" speech to him. I appreciated the gesture, but honestly, I don't remember being that hurt by what he did. When my age was still in the single digits, stuttering wasn't a major issue for me. I was more focused on my favorite action heroes, the Teenage Mutant Ninja Turtles.

My mother and oldest brother also stuttered when they were younger, but they underwent unconventional means of speech therapy: My grandmother yelled and demanded that my mother stop stuttering (her form of shock therapy). It worked.

My brother got over his stuttering by listening to professionals on TV and mimicking how they pronounced and enunciated words, and projected their voices.

My parents never took me to a doctor for my stuttering, but my moms arranged for me to start speech therapy in 4th grade.

My speech therapy sessions, which were about a class period long, were designed for the children in school who had speech difficulties. My exercises included saying a list of common phrases like "Hello, how are you doing?" and reading a piece of writing aloud to practice getting rid of the stutter.

I think the exercises would've been more effective if I'd taken them more seriously. I didn't practice at home and barely used what I had learned when speaking to someone outside my speech therapy sessions. My parents didn't push me because they trusted me to handle all my school-related business. Since I didn't practice much, I kept stuttering. As I got into middle school I started to feel aggravated and disappointed.

My dad, understanding my frustration, gave me a second opportunity to cure my speech difficulties when I was about 12. He taught me a rhythmic breathing exercise he'd learned from a musician friend. I had to sit with my eyes closed and breathe in and out according to a specific pattern, following along with African music.

My dad guaranteed that if I practiced 30 minutes a day for a month or two, it would eventually eliminate my problem. After several weeks, my stammering had greatly decreased. I still stuttered occasionally, but not as much as before.

But after about a month, I fell off track and didn't do the breathing exercises consistently. After coming down with a case of the "I don't feel like its," skipping one day turned into not doing it at all. My stuttering returned gradually over the next few weeks, and I've been cursed ever since.

Now, light years later, when I want to share something with someone, like a joke or some personal poetry—or even say my own name—and I can't get the words out, I feel frustrated and inhibited. I get a bad emotional taste in my mouth.

It's like there's a parasite inside me with a mind of its own, causing my speech—and sometimes my entire body—to go in directions I don't want it to. As a result, I've gotten shyer as I've gotten older. And when I do speak, I speak with a low voice so that people can't hear in case I stammer.

"Speak up, I can't hear you!" complain family, friends, and coworkers. Oh, how I hate to repeat myself. I said it as good as biscuits the first time, but they didn't hear me. So I've got to do it over, and risk stuttering.

Most people don't ridicule me, at least not to my face. But I've heard a friend's mother and an older male relative make jokes and do imitations of my stammer. Sometimes I know or suspect people have said something behind my back. I feel embarrassed and a little small when they do it.

My stutter makes me feel abnormal. So why haven't I continued to take my "medicine," the exercises that are my saving grace? Maybe I've been wishing I'd just grow out of it.

Not being able to get myself to consistently fight against the stuttering makes me feel like I'm too weak to overcome my speech impediment. My stuttering and my lack of commitment to reach my goal have been the most aggravating issues in my life.

I finally realized a few months ago that things won't change unless I take necessary steps to change them.

I finally realized a few months ago that things won't change unless I take necessary steps to change them. I'm tired of stuttering and I really believe, for the first time, that it's not too late to work on it. I want the things I say to be understood clearly and completely. I have things inside me that need proper verbal expression.

If I want to follow my dream to become an artist and lecturer, I need to speak clearly. I can imagine giving lectures to impressionable college students about my art, writing, and personal philosophy, and maybe even interviewing my favorite celebrities. But I can't get my James Lipton on—(he's the host of the TV show *Inside the Actor's Studio)* if I speak like Porky Pig.

So I'm back to doing the breathing exercises regularly again.

I've promised myself to do the exercises every day, in the morning when I wake up and before I go to bed, for 30 minutes at a time. In the last few weeks, I've stuck to my plan every day except one.

Now I'm not stuttering as much anymore, and I feel so elated. I can't wait until it's gone. I want to become recognized for my artwork and writing instead of my stutter. I'm dreaming big dreams now, seeing myself touring colleges nationwide and speaking to youth, making them laugh, shocking them, and inspiring them with the basic message of doing what's best for themselves.

I'll be happy when I'm speaking and it sounds like a CD without the scratches.

Gamal was 20 when he wrote this story.
He works as a pre-school teacher.

Gamal Jones

Why People Stutter

By Gamal Jones

I wanted to get a professional perspective on stuttering, so I interviewed Catherine Montgomery, executive director of the American Institute for Stuttering in Manhattan.

Q: What is stuttering?

A: It's the result of the vocal cords closing off when you want to talk. The brain signals don't coordinate properly to get the vocal cords vibrating at exactly the right time. So the vocal cords spasm, sound won't come out, and people push hard and struggle to make the sounds come out. That's what most people hear as stuttering.

When the vocal cords are closed or spasming, the human response is to do something to stay alive because your airway is closing off, so you push and squeeze and your breathing gets all thrown off. That's why so many people who may see you struggling say, "Come on, breathe."

It's a disorder that fluctuates. Like asthma, sometimes it's worse than other times. It can be made worse by things like stress or anxiety.

Q: When does stuttering usually start?

A: It usually starts between the ages of 2 and 5.

Q: Why do people stutter?

A: It's inherited, which means it's passed down through the genes within families. It has to do with some brain signals that don't signal the speech muscles the right way. It's really a physical thing.

Q: Do stutterers have any specific personality traits?

A: It's not related to personality. It's a genetic disorder that affects about 1% of the world's population. It affects four times as many males as females. It's not the personality that helps create the stuttering, but [the other way around]. Certain characteristics like being shy or quiet develop as a result of dealing with your stuttering.

Q: Many stutterers often stutter when they say their names. Why is saying my own name so difficult?

A: It's common for stutterers to stutter on specific words, like one's name, or in specific situations or with particular people. This is the learned aspect of stuttering. In other words, you have trouble saying your name once, so the next time someone asks your name, you remember the trouble. That memory triggers more tension and the difficulty happens again.

Q: What should someone who stutters do if he knows he's about to stutter?

A: Without professional help, the most powerful thing you can do for yourself is to acknowledge your stuttering to your listener. Have an acceptance of your stuttering. Even have a sense of humor about it. I call it self-advertising. Give your listener a heads up: "Hey I stutter sometimes. Hang on, hang in there with me."

Stuttering is a physical, genetic disorder that affects about 1% of the world's population.

Folks who stutter have spent most of their time trying not to stutter, and trying to hide. I think it's an awesome concept to think about just being open about it, and people find it so liberating. It's a natural instinct to look away when you're in the midst of stuttering. But with eye contact, you keep your listener engaged and you also demonstrate what appears to be more confidence.

Q: Are there ways to get rid of stuttering?

A: If we get kids who are 2 to 5 years old, it can be eradicated if the right things are done. We can treat the stuttering before the neurological systems get hard wired. Early intervention is really important in stuttering.

For stutterers who are school age through adult age, it's not going to be gotten rid of. But people can learn to manage it so it doesn't rule their lives. And yes, people can learn to speak a heck of a lot more fluently and easily. It's possible to learn how to coordinate your vocal cords if you work with an experienced therapist.

Q: How should a non-stutterer communicate with a stutterer?

A: Communicate in a normal, natural way. Do not fill in words for them—but that's not a 100% rule either. I've had people actually say, "I really like it when people fill in my words for me." But the majority say, "I don't like when people do that." Don't assume you know what that word is going to be. Be a patient listener. Make natural eye contact.

Q: Is there anything that you would like to add?

A: Those who stutter are, on average, 14 points higher in IQ than the normal population. Studies have been done that show this, but I don't know why it's true.

Gamal was 20 when he wrote this story.

Skyler Kane Kraemer

Will the Tortoise Win the Race?

By Eric Green

Everybody says you need to graduate from high school to succeed in life. But what if you just can't pass your classes? Should you keep trying? I'm 20 years old and I'm still in the 11th grade. I failed 9th grade once and failed 10th grade three times. I'm not sure I'll ever graduate.

Until 9th grade, I was in special education classes. In elementary school, I felt like the smartest kid in the class. I was a straight-A student. In junior high, I constantly got 100s on spelling quizzes, and sometimes made the honor roll.

In 6th grade, I started to have trouble for the first time. When my math teacher called me up to the board to solve a problem, I was the slowest one to finish in the whole class. Some of my teachers yelled and screamed at me. One teacher called me "slow" and "stupid." I began to hate her and think of myself as stupid. On good days, I'd tell myself, "I'm smart, just not as quick as other people."

In the 9th grade, I got switched to regular classes and went to the resource room for extra help. In my regular classes, students talked down to kids in special ed., calling us slow. I'd think, "That's where you're wrong. I go to resource room because I have a learning disability, and I'm willing to get as much help as possible." But I kept my mouth shut because I didn't want to get teased even more.

That year, my biological mom died. My mind was not on school at all. Suddenly school was too hard. I seemed to have lost my ability to understand the work. I began to think I was not intelligent enough to pass high school classes. I would sit in class looking at the assignment while everyone else completed theirs.

Sometimes when I took an assignment seriously I'd do well. Then I'd feel proud and confident. Most of the time, though, I'd become overwhelmed and frustrated. Once, in math class, I got extra help and did all of my assignments. When I got my report card, I saw that my math teacher had given me a 65.

I'd feel stupid any time I tried to complete a difficult task. I stopped believing that I could ever pass.

"Why did you give me a 65?" I asked him.

"You didn't do well on the exams," he said.

I was furious. Didn't he know I was working as hard as I could? Didn't he understand how it feels to try hard but not be rewarded or recognized? I thought I deserved a better grade because of my effort, even if I couldn't do well on the tests.

Situations like that made me feel neglected by my teachers. Growing up, my parents and my first foster parent neglected me. My biological parents would disappear without a trace and leave my siblings and me in the house for hours. They didn't seem to notice who I was or what I needed.

I felt the same way when my teachers overlooked the efforts I made, or stood by while other kids in the class teased me and called me names. I felt that some of my teachers did not want to deal with me anymore and didn't pay attention to me when I asked for help. I felt lonely and isolated and stuck with problems that I couldn't solve.

*E*ventually, I stopped asking for help. I'd feel stupid any time I tried to complete a difficult task. I stopped believing that I could ever pass, even if I got all the extra help in the world. I thought I'd never be a successful person.

Then I began to refuse to do class work. I'd spend my time writing poems or drawing pictures—two things I know I'm good at. When the teacher asked me about the assignment I was supposed to be doing, I'd have nothing to show.

I hoped that my teachers would notice that I was angry, or lost. But when I took my adoptive mother, Lorine, to my parent-teacher conferences, my teachers only seemed frustrated.

One teacher told her, "Eric is a very talented poet and artist, but he doesn't do the work that is required of him. He just sits in the back of the classroom and writes his poems. He is very inattentive and uncooperative. He's a nice young man. I know he can do better."

Lorine said, "You see, that's the same exact thing that I be telling him. He gets mad and starts to cop an attitude. He doesn't like to study, or do his homework. Every day he just comes home and sits on the floor and draws and writes poems."

Every teacher we met told my mother the same thing. Even my art teacher, whose class is my favorite, told her, "Eric is not paying attention in class; he does not do the assignments. Eric does what he wants to do."

I felt embarrassed because it was the truth. One day in my art class, the task was to draw a still life of a bowl of fruit. While the rest of the class was drawing the fruit, I was doing my own drawings, because I only like to draw self-portraits, cartoon characters, and washing machines.

I knew that I should do what was asked of me instead of being troublesome. But when Lorine asked me why I wouldn't cooperate with my teachers, I was too embarrassed to come out with the reason for my behavior—that I felt like a failure. So I said, "I believe that school should suit my interests. I don't understand how learning math will help me become a poet or an artist!"

Finally, the anxiety and the feeling of wasting my life got to be too much. I told my mother, "I am dropping out."

"If you decide to drop out of high school, then you can leave this house and live with someone else," Lorine said.

Luckily, my counselor helped me transfer to a smaller high school where I could get more attention. I thought that in a better environment I would do better in school and be able to go forward in life. At first, I was more focused and willing to do the work. The teachers went out of their way to help me, and the students were respectful and easy to get along with.

My counselor also explained to me that having a learning disability is different from being dumb. "When you're a smart person with a learning disability, you can master an academic curriculum if you have plenty of assistance and you work hard. A dumb person is one who is unwilling to participate in classes or stick to the curriculum," she said.

I hoped that my teachers would notice that I was angry, or lost. But they only seemed frustrated.

Lately, though, I've run into some new obstacles. In New York, you have to pass certain exams to graduate. I've taken some of those exams—in history and English—and I've failed all of them, some more than once.

Last year, I was looking through my file and I found out that I'd been diagnosed with Fetal Alcohol Syndrome. I looked that up on the Internet and found out that it's a problem affecting children whose mothers drank a lot while they were pregnant. It listed these characteristics:

—difficulty getting along with friends and family
—mental retardation
—growth deficiencies
—behavior problems
—incomplete education

Looking at the list, I thought to myself, "Do those traits describe me? Is there something wrong with me?"

I felt depressed. I feared that I might never be a normal student and might never graduate from high school. I felt angry that my biological mother drank (I remember her drinking when I lived with her). I also worried that my brothers might have the same thing.

I went home and told Lorine what I had read and how I felt. She refused to believe it. She told me, "Eric, you're smart and you should not use that diagnosis as an excuse."

I also told some of my teachers, who told me, "You need to have confidence in your abilities. You have potential and the intelligence to succeed. You're smart, creative, artistic, and unique. You write beautiful poetry. Do not punish yourself like that, Eric. Believe in yourself."

Right now, I'm not sure what to believe about myself. Some days I feel smart and hopeful, other days I'm discouraged. On those days, I don't even try to work toward graduation. I just sit in my classes, drawing and writing poetry. Those are my talents, and when I look at the words and pictures I've created, I feel like it doesn't matter if I succeed in high school or not.

Still, if I don't graduate, I'll feel like a fool for letting myself and my family and friends down. I'm a smart person, I want to succeed, and everybody's in my corner. My friends tell me, "Your mother is right to be upset with you. You need an education." My mom tells me, "I want to see you with that paper in your hand."

I want to see that, too.

Eric was 20 when he wrote this story. The following year, he succeeded in graduating from high school.

Evelyn Brzezinska

A Classmate in a Wheelchair

By Esther Rajavelu

I first saw him freshman year, rolling by in his wheelchair through the halls of my specialty science high school. His short arms rested on the desktop attached to his chair. He had dark hair, a frozen smile, and he stared straight ahead. He didn't seem to look anyone in the eye. "They let people like that in Brooklyn Tech?" I thought.

One day, I was standing in the hall with some other kids waiting for our history class to begin when he rolled up. I felt myself stiffen and I wanted to get away from him, but I couldn't. I didn't want to hurt his feelings by moving, but I didn't want to embarrass myself by being seen next to him. I had the urge to say something, but my mind was blank.

Finally, I glanced at him and decided to smile. He looked at me as if I were a ghost and tried to smile back. That surprised me.

I thought he would just ignore me. I quickly looked away wishing the teacher would come, so I could rush into class.

Then I noticed everybody else was quiet too. It hit me that I wasn't the only one who felt creepy when he was around. Nearly everyone's attitude changed when he entered class. The chatter stopped and kids looked the other way. Even the teachers ignored him. It was like they wanted to erase him from the class. I wondered what was behind this "weird" feeling.

I began to realize how uncomfortable and afraid I feel around disabled people. After all, before high school, the only people I ever saw in wheelchairs were in the movies. Because I didn't really know anyone who was disabled, I got all my ideas from family, friends, and TV.

I definitely believe that the stories I've heard about disabled people influenced the way I felt around them. For instance, the day I smiled at the boy in the wheelchair, I came home and told my mom about it.

"I don't know why he looked at me so weird," I said.

"Well, he probably felt uncomfortable in his position," my mom said. "I don't think it's a good idea for you to get too friendly with him. People like that could get possessive because they're always lonely, and he might try and take advantage of you." Then she told me she read a magazine article about a disabled man who killed his best friend for wanting to spend less time together.

That made me think twice about becoming friends with him. For most of the next year, I listened to my mom's advice. Whenever the boy in the wheelchair was around, I just ignored him. If I saw him in the hall or in class, I turned my head. I would have kept it up if something hadn't happened that made me wonder why I was so afraid of him.

My junior year, I was walking around my government class selling candy bars for the debate team, but nobody was buying. When I walked past the boy in the wheelchair, I heard a murmur that sounded like a request for candy. I was so shocked that I wasn't even sure if he had spoken.

I stood there gaping for a moment and then handed him two bars. From under his desk he got two dollars and gave it to me. I walked back to my desk in amazement.

I tried to be very honest about my feelings and stereotypes, and I asked a lot of questions.

Later, I realized that when I was going around the class-room asking everybody else if they wanted candy, I hadn't even thought to ask him. I just didn't think he ate candy, or anything else that my friends and I liked. I thought he was too different.

After this, I really wanted to learn how to act around him. A part of me wanted to be extra-friendly, but in my heart I knew I would feel like a fraud. Even now, I'm afraid of what my friends might think if I started hanging out with him. But ignoring him didn't work either, because I still felt uncomfortable whenever he was around.

I started to deal with that "weird" feeling I get around disabled people. I tried to be very honest about my feelings and stereotypes, and I asked a lot of questions. I think it paid off, because my attitude began to change a little. Now I know there's more to being around people with disabilities than feeling pity.

Esther was 17 when she wrote this story. She went to college and graduate school and works for a financial company.

Nicole Rice

From Sore Loser to MVP

By Michelle Stallworth

When you think of basketball, what comes to mind? Seven-foot-tall guys running up and down the court making fast breaks? Well, I'm a 5'2" girl in a wheelchair, but I also play. Here's how it happened.

I grew up with seven cousins and they always used to ask me to go outside and play baseball, basketball, or whatever. I would always refuse because in order to play I would have to put away my braces and use my wheelchair. And I hated the wheelchair because I thought it made me look handicapped. (I had an accident when I was a year old. I can walk with braces but to play sports I need to keep my hands free, so I have to use my chair.)

I had watched a few games with my cousins, but the games were too long and boring for me. I didn't understand the rules. And the only players I liked were the ones I thought were cute.

Then when I got to middle school I had a gym teacher, Mr. Hill, who really encouraged me. He had coached a college basketball team, and also helped organize events for the Special Olympics. A lot of teachers were uncomfortable and fake around physically challenged kids, but he seemed comfortable and cool.

One day while my gym class was learning basketball, he told me, "You have long fingers. You should either learn basketball or the piano," and I took him seriously.

I had never really thought about playing sports before. Because I was self-conscious about using my wheelchair, I spent a lot of time by myself, inside the house. I liked to be the best at whatever I did and I hadn't thought about being really good at anything besides writing, which was something I did often. After Mr. Hill's comment, I thought, "I don't like piano, so why not try basketball?"

Mr. Hill taught me how to dribble and how to shoot pretty well. He told me if I kept practicing maybe I could play basketball in the Special Olympics someday. After he told me that I made it one of my goals. One day when I was in the school lunchroom, I told a staff member that I hoped to play in a five-on-five game against really good wheelchair players in the Special Olympics.

A lot of teachers were uncomfortable and fake around physically challenged kids, but Mr. Hill seemed comfortable and cool.

A girl who was a good friend of mine overheard what I said and whispered to another friend, "Can you imagine a bunch of crippled people playing basketball?" The guy she was talking to started acting like he was retarded and trying to dribble a ball.

I didn't want anyone to know how hurt I was, so I didn't say anything. I just laughed like everyone else. But after that, I wanted to prove what a good player I could be. I couldn't wait to go to high school and get the chance to play on a real team.

Fortunately, my high school had a group of students that

was interested in starting a wheelchair basketball team. I hadn't played very much on a team before, and there were some things I had to work on. I couldn't play defense, for one. Even worse, I was a sore loser.

I was at my worst during a game we played against Hillcrest High School about a year ago. We started the game without our center, Thomas, who decided he didn't want to play because of an argument he was having with the coach. Thomas was 6'3" and a great ball-handler. He was our star, and it hurt us not to have him.

I was the best player after Thomas, so I thought I was supposed to carry the team in his absence. Throughout the game, my teammates would pass me the ball as soon as they got it; the opposing players double- and triple-teamed me.

I didn't know what to do so I either lost the ball or threw up shots that hit nothing but bottom (that is, they hit the bottom of the net without going through the hoop first). Once, I was all alone under the basket and missed an easy lay-up. I got fouled a couple of times, but I missed all my free throws. I even got hit in the head by a pass.

During one play, my teammate Lamont told me to go by the basket and he would pass me the ball. But first, he passed it to another player, James, who passed it back to him. Then Lamont threw it back to James and it slipped out of his hands. They managed to get the ball back and while I wasn't looking Lamont passed it to me. But where did the ball go? Off my head and out of bounds—it was Hillcrest's ball now.

I started getting really mad and screaming at my teammates, even though I was really mad at myself. I was the point guard and it was my job to score and get my teammates involved. I started hogging the ball, but as soon as I did that, the coach called a time out.

She called me over to the bench, and then she screamed at me. "Pass the ball!" she said. "People are getting open." So I went back in and passed the ball to a teammate. He caught the pass, but missed the shot. I just looked at the whole team with a vicious stare.

The next time Coach called a time out, I stayed on the court instead of going into the huddle. Coach just looked at me and said I was a crybaby who couldn't handle pressure.

From that point on, everything just got worse. A boy on the Hillcrest team actually pushed me out of my chair and the ref didn't call a foul. In fact, the ref gave his team the ball! Things didn't get much better after that. We lost the game, 33 to 12.

I spent a lot of time last summer playing with the walkers (able-bodied people) around my way.

After the game, I walked out on my team. I hated everyone on it. I thought they were all scrubs. The teachers who came to support us said I was a baby and a sore loser. It took me a while to calm down and finally admit that I was one of five people who had played horribly. I hoped never to have another game like that. I also hoped we'd get to play Hillcrest again so we could get even.

I knew I needed to practice if I was going to improve my game so nothing like that would ever happen again. So I spent a lot of time last summer playing with the walkers (able-bodied people) around my way. We played in the school gyms that were open and outside at the playground. I also thought about playing on the street courts near where I lived, but I thought the guys would make fun of me. Finally I just decided to give it a try.

I went over to the court and a few guys were shooting around. At first things were a little scary and I was reluctant to join in. But I asked if I could play, and the guys said OK.

After a little shooting around, I caught fire. I was the only wheelchair player on the court, but every time I would touch the ball they would tell me to shoot it, and that gave me confidence. When one game I was playing became tied, a kid named Shawn said, "You're gonna get the last shot." He passed the ball to me when I got open under the basket and although a defender was on me, I shot the ball under his arms and it rolled in.

After that I went outside to play with the guys almost every day for the rest of the summer. Then, when school started, I got to practice regularly with my wheelchair team, and during the regular season we developed a better team chemistry than we had the previous year.

In many games this year, Thomas and I had a kind of two-man dominance. I learned that all I could do was play my best and pass the ball when I felt I should. But the other players would still pass to me a lot and I learned it was OK to take the shot when I had it. I became very confident in my game. After a good regular season, we found ourselves playing in the championships. Against who? Who else? Hillcrest.

Everyone was saying my team had no skills because of the way we played last year, so I came into the game thinking I had something to prove. During the first half, we got no respect. A scrub talked trash to me and made me so mad that I lost my concentration. But the second half was a different story.

The announcer started calling out my name: "Michelle steals the ball from Alex; she has a 2-on-1 break," he said. I faked a shot and made a no-look pass to my teammate and the announcer went, "Another beautiful pass by Michelle Stallworth."

Hearing my name called out like that made me light up. I started pumping my fist, and the girls in the crowd from Hillcrest were telling their team, "Watch the girl, she's mad quick."

My teammates were blocking for me so I could get open shots. At one point, I got ahead of everybody on a fast break. Three defenders chased after me but never caught up.

On defense, I blocked a three-point shot by Hillcrest's all-star point guard, who is considered the best point guard in the city. When the final buzzer sounded, it turned out to be the best game I had ever played. I scored 18 points, had seven rebounds, seven assists and seven steals. And best of all, we beat Hillcrest, 29 to 17.

After the game, Hillcrest's principal came over and told me that I was the best player on the court. The announcer called my name as the Most Valuable Player. On my way out, a group of boys from Hillcrest started yelling "MVP!" Then they said, "You play mad good, Shorty. Keep your head up."

For the next three days, I was the most conceited person you would ever want to meet. But then it seemed like people were forgetting about my teammates while they kept congratulating me. I realized it wasn't fair—James, Edgar, and Chipell had played great too. I had to regain my head and tell everybody who gave me credit that our win was a team effort.

My teammates seemed jealous about all the attention I was getting. Since I was the only girl on the team, I said to them, laughing, "What's the matter? Y'all mad because the girl is getting all the attention?"

I was joking but I knew deep down in my heart that it wasn't a game without them. I'll always remember that game and the pizza party we had afterwards.

Playing basketball relieves a lot of tension for me. All my worries disappear when I'm on the court.

I am very thankful to basketball because it taught me how to socialize with other people and make friends. It's helped me to not be so shy. I don't worry as much about people criticizing me or making fun of me because I'm in a wheelchair. It also forced me to face some things about myself, from my quick temper to the fact that I'm a sore loser. I'm more in control of those things now.

Playing basketball relieves a lot of tension for me too. All my worries disappear when I'm on the court; nothing is on my mind but winning.

Some of my friends have encouraged me to make playing in the NBA a goal, but I don't want to be the only wheelchair player in the NBA. I can't shake the feeling that people might look at me in some weird way, like that girl back in junior high school. I imagine that I would get a lot of criticism every time I missed a shot or couldn't guard somebody, and I couldn't take that. Playing in the NBA is hard enough for walkers. For me, it would be a living nightmare.

What I am thinking about doing is writing a letter to the commissioner of the NBA. I'm thinking of asking him: Why not make a league for wheelchair players too?

Michelle was 17 when she wrote this story.

Edward Cortez

Would Freeing My Speech Change My Life?

By Donald Moore

Can you say "three?" Seems like a silly question, doesn't it? Who can't say it? Well, until a few months ago, I couldn't. I had a condition known as ankyloglossia, better known as tongue-tie, which meant the tip of my tongue was connected to the bottom of my mouth.

Everyone's tongue is connected to the bottom of the mouth by the frenulum, a short piece of flexible tissue underneath the tongue. For most people, the frenulum is unnoticeable unless you lift your tongue to the roof of your mouth. But for me, it reached almost to the front of my tongue, so that I could barely lift my tongue.

That meant I couldn't move my tongue between my lips or against my teeth, the way most people do when they speak. Even though it wasn't painful or uncomfortable, it did affect how I talked. Most noticeably, I mispronounced the "thr" sound as "fr."

On the first day of 1st grade, I made a conscious effort not to say any word containing the "thr" sound. I'd planned it all out before school. If I had to tell someone the time, "3:33" would become "27 to 4:00." "Threw" would become "tossed" or "launched." And if I ever got a sore throat, I'd just say neck.

For some reason, I thought that if I made it through the first day, the rest of the year would be a breeze. And it almost worked, too. I lasted all the way until recess. I was playing with several other children on the monkey bars when I made the mistake of saying "through" several times without realizing it. One boy noticed.

"Say through," he said.

And my cover was blown. If I'd known any swear words back then, I probably would have used them. The rest of recess was spent with kids (most of whom would become my friends) playing speech therapist. If only I could say "three," they figured. The other words would be easy. "Say three," they said.

"Free," I said.

A collective groan from the other kids. "No, three."

It might have been funny to an onlooker, but it was annoying to me. They kept badgering me, when I knew that I simply couldn't do it, no matter how

My friends' curiosity about my tongue-tie changed to teasing.

good their coaching was. I was embarrassed that their first impression of me was of a kid who couldn't say his numbers right.

Luckily, 6-year-olds' attention spans are short, and after we went back inside, no one brought it up again. Until, of course, I'd try to say the word "three" again.

This went on for the rest of 1st and 2nd grades, until I changed schools. Sometime during those two years, my friends' curiosity about my tongue-tie changed to teasing. It was never a "Ha ha, his tongue's weird, don't talk to him" kind of teasing, but more of a "Ha ha, his tongue's weird, let's play with him" sort of thing. I never had trouble making or keeping friends.

But in middle school, I started liking girls. Having girls tease me was worse than guys doing it. I imagined some vast middle school girl plot to spread news of my tongue-tie and prevent me from getting a girlfriend.

Luckily, things changed quite a bit in high school. For one thing, the name of my high school didn't have the "thr" sound in it, which had been an unfortunate coincidence with all my old schools: PS 183, PS 3 and IS 383. Plus, there were so many students, with so many different classes, that the only way anyone could've known I had tongue-tie is if I told them, or when I had to read a long passage out loud in class.

But the ones who did know raised the teasing to a whole new level of sophistication. My favorite example: "What's Donald's idea of purgatory? Having to completely divide one by three." (One divided by three equals .333 followed by an infinite number of threes.) It was funny—the first time I heard it. The two dozen other times? Kind of annoying. After a while, I learned to ignore it.

I'd be lying if I said I was fine with it, though. It was frustrating having to speak loudly and enunciate especially well just so people could understand me. For a guy who didn't wear glasses and wasn't short, overweight, or poor, a minor speech impediment seemed like the worst thing in the world. I always thought that if it weren't for that one thing, no one would have anything to tease me about.

And it didn't help when, this past September, I started feeling sharp pains in the tip of my tongue. At first I thought I'd bitten it in my sleep. When a week passed and the pain was still there, I decided to go with my mom to see a doctor.

"Your frenulum's tearing," the doctor said.

"Huh?" I said.

The doctor smiled. "Your frenulum. It's what connects the tongue to the bottom of your mouth. You have tongue-tie, so it's much more prominent. And it's tearing."

The fear must've shown on my face, because he assured me that it was nothing serious. It would heal completely in about a week, or I could have an operation to have my tongue-tie fixed. When he said this, my spirits rose.

I always thought that if it weren't for that one thing, no one would have anything to tease me about.

The last time my parents had seriously considered getting my tongue-tie fixed was when I was an infant. That's when most children have it corrected, but I was sick with an ear infection after I was born. So the doctor had suggested waiting to see if my tongue-tie caused any complications with breast feeding or breathing. It never did, and by the time I was speaking, my parents didn't think the operation was worth the risk.

The idea of surgery had crossed my mind a lot growing up. But I'd always seen it as a cosmetic operation involving lots of time and money, not to mention pain and recovery time, just so I could pronounce some words better. It didn't seem worth it. Now that I had a good reason to have it done, it was a pretty easy decision. I wanted the surgery as soon as possible.

A week later, my dad drove my mom and me to the hospital for what I thought would be a pre-surgery appointment. Then the doctor told us it could be done that day, right away. My first reaction was disbelief—surely it couldn't be that easy. "How long will the procedure take?" I asked.

"About 15 minutes," he said. Part of me was nervous, but the other part, the part that ultimately won, told me to go ahead with it.

And so I ended up in one of those chairs they have at dentists' offices with a blue napkin clipped to my neck. While the doctor was preparing for the operation, my eyes began wandering around the room. The walls were covered with posters, diagrams of the mouth and teeth, and pictures of oral disfigurements and conditions.

One particular poster caught my eye. It showed an African boy with a cleft lip. A cleft lip is when a person's lip doesn't fully form when developing inside the womb, leaving a large split in the upper lip. This boy had a particularly bad cleft. The split was so big it seemed as if his upper lip rose up to meet his nose, leaving his gums and teeth visible. My first feeling was revulsion.

Then I started to think about the boy. I thought about how much his life was going to be impacted by his cleft lip. Not only was he horribly disfigured, but unless he had surgery, he was going to be singled out because of how he looked for the rest of his life.

Compared to him, my tongue-tie seemed downright trivial. All I had to deal with was the occasional mispronounced word or taunt from one of my peers. Was it that big a deal?

Before I had time to answer that question, the doctor came in. He injected the inside of my mouth with something and asked, "Can you feel anything?" I answered yes several times, but in a couple of minutes the anesthetic had taken effect.

I kept my eyes open during it all, and I saw the doctor coming toward me with an eight-inch-long pair of scissors to snip my problem away. I had an initial moment of fear—what if I do feel it?—and then anticipation, waiting for it to be finished so I could see and feel the results. Then, almost as soon as the doctor started, he was done.

Afterwards, he told me to try pronouncing some words, including, yes, the number three. I found that I could, with some effort. (At least, that's what the doctor told me—to this day I still hear no difference between the "fr" and "thr" sounds.) I was a new man. Or so I thought.

Later that day, I contacted my friends online to tell them about the surgery. They were less than impressed. I'd never bothered to tell many of them that I had tongue-tie, and some were surprised to hear about it. "I just thought it was your accent," a few of them said.

"What accent?" I wondered. I knew my friends had heard my mom's Southern accent before. Did they blame my vocal flaws on a Southern accent too, even though I've lived in New York all my life? I was puzzled.

"I've been teased and made fun of most of my life because of this," I thought, "and now no one even cares that it's fixed." I even tried surefire conversation pieces—before and after pictures of my mouth that I took with my camera phone. Still no "Hooray Donald!" like I'd been expecting.

"I've been teased and made fun of most of my life because of this," I thought, "and now no one even cares that it's fixed."

And my family? They were mostly annoyed I was eating all the ice cream because I couldn't eat solid food for two days. For a while, I tried to do tricks to impress them, and to justify my operation to myself. All the things I couldn't do before became goals of mine.

Whistling? Not much luck.

Saying the "thr" sound? Yes, with about a minute of preparation time. I had to consciously move my tongue to where it needed to be since I'd never done it before.

Sticking out my tongue? Yeah, but how useful is that?

By the end of that first day, I realized that my surgery hadn't drastically changed my life. My family hardly cared that it was fixed and half my friends hadn't even noticed my tongue-tie to begin with. Had tongue-tie really been that big of a problem?

Now, several months later, I'm even more convinced that my problem was insignificant compared to that African boy with the cleft lip. It never stopped me from making friends or living a normal life.

In a way, what happened was a bit like peer pressure. I wanted to have the operation so I could be like everyone else. My friends, my classmates, even my sister, all shaped my view of what I should be, without even consciously trying. But in the end, the only person telling me to change was me.

I don't regret having the operation. But I do realize that the effect tongue-tie had on me came mostly from my own mind. I made a big deal out of it for years because I assumed it was a big deal to other people. In reality, it wasn't. I fit in now just as well as I did before, regardless of whether I can say "three" or not.

Donald was 18 when he wrote this story. He later attended college, majoring in writing and literature.

D. Alen Michaeilov

Listen, and I'll Learn

By Zizi Lavada Baity

For a long time, education was not something that I liked, and I didn't think it was very important in my life. When I was growing up, it sometimes seemed like the only thing I was learning in school was that I wasn't learning anything.

When I was in 3rd grade, my mother had me transferred to a new school because I was always getting into trouble. As soon as I got there, I knew that I didn't want to be there. I wanted to be in my old school, which was racially mixed, with my old friends. I was the only black girl in my class, and there were only two other black students in the entire school. Right away I felt uncomfortable.

Because I didn't want to be there, I became the class clown. I knew that the more trouble I got into, the faster I would be writing my ticket out of there. I really wasn't a loud class clown. I have always been like I am now, shy. Instead, I would make faces at the teacher or make quiet jokes. To be honest, it took my teacher, Ms. Ross, a good couple of months to figure out that I could talk.

I had a real problem talking to grown-ups. In more than one way, not communicating made it harder for me to learn. I would never talk to any of my teachers. When I didn't understand what was being taught, I would write or doodle. I never asked for help.

I also didn't do the work that was given out. I couldn't deal with admitting it was too hard for me. I felt that it was easier to give up without even trying. I'd ask my mother for help, but after she tried her best to explain the work, I still couldn't grasp it. She would get frustrated and tell me that I knew the work and I was just fooling around.

She'd say, "Ask your teacher. It's her job to teach you, anyway."

But when I asked Ms. Ross, she told me I should have paid attention in class, and I should figure it out on my own. And because I didn't understand the work, I just fooled around in class more.

To make matters worse, I sat next to a girl who made me miserable. When Margaret first sat next to me, she would kick me and then say that she was sorry. She would do it over and over again, until my leg was numb.

Then came the name-calling. She'd start out, "Hey, n-gger b-tch..." She also told me that I had no right being there and that black people should have gone back to Africa when they had the chance. When I didn't listen to her, she'd say, "Don't worry. You'll hear me later on, in the girls' room." And sure enough she would find me and beat me up no matter what bathroom I was in.

When she called me names, I didn't know how to react. At

first I was in shock. As she kept doing it, I began to feel empty, like I lost something. It was my self-esteem. Hearing someone say, "You are worthless and don't deserve to be here" every day doesn't make you feel good about yourself.

How do I put this? You could shrug it off if you heard it only a few times. But when someone is constantly drilling it inside your head, it's like you have no choice but to believe it. I used to think sometimes, "Damn, if she's saying it so much, it must be true."

It made things worse that no one seemed to care about how I felt. Sometimes I'd raise my hand to tell Ms. Ross that Margaret was bothering me. Ms. Ross would ask Margaret, "Is that true?" Margaret would say no, and Ms. Ross would tell me to stop wasting her time.

It sometimes seemed like the only thing I was learning in school was that I wasn't learning anything.

This is why I never bothered to complain: No one ever listened to what I had to say. Maybe I should have complained louder, or made a point of telling someone what was going on over and over again. Eventually I did defend myself against Margaret. One day in the courtyard after lunch she called me n-gger.

"Don't you get bored of calling me that?" I said. I knew what I was doing. I was picking a fight. "Don't you have anything new to say to me, huh?"

Then I slapped her, and Margaret ran after me, yelling at the top of her lungs, "I'm going to get you, n-gger."

I guess in all the fuss she didn't notice that she ran past Mr. June, the principal. It was my lucky day. He took Margaret to his office. I'm not sure what he said to her, but after that, Margaret lightened up on the name-calling. It made me feel good to finally have someone take my problems seriously.

One of the best things I did for myself after that was to finally speak up. I eventually got on the right track by telling people what I needed. One day I told Mr. June that I didn't understand the work. I found it hard. So he recommended that I be tested for special education.

A woman tested me and assigned me to leave class and learn in a resource room in the morning. Resource was fun. The teacher broke down everything so it was easier to understand. Soon, because I was learning so much, my attitude toward education changed. I began to enjoy school because I was able to keep up. Every morning my resource teacher would have a hard time getting me to leave because I wanted to stay and learn some more. I liked it there.

*E*ventually I changed schools so I could be in a special education class all day, instead of just going in the morning. And once I got to my new school, my mother was very happy because I was behaving myself and getting good grades for the first time since kindergarten.

Getting good grades made me feel that I could handle school, and I wanted to be there. The learning was at a slow pace, so I knew I could keep up. It gave me a lot more confidence. Before that I thought I could not learn.

My new school was also racially mixed, which made me feel a lot more comfortable.

I was excited, but I didn't know then it was going to be a long year. By the time Christmas vacation was over, our teacher had left and she never came back.

Our class was stuck without a teacher for months. Once we had a substitute teacher, but she only lasted for one day. The class was just bouncing off the walls. We had this set of checkers, and the boys took all the pieces and threw them all over the hallway and down the stairs. The poor woman couldn't get us to stop yelling or sit down, and half of the class was missing.

After that, no substitute wanted to take us. Sometimes Ms. Santana, a teacher who taught upstairs, would take me and another girl and let us stay in her class. In her class, we could actually learn. The principal would come down the hall to tell me this wasn't my class; my class was down the hall. But I spoke up. I told him I didn't want to stay in a class with no teacher.

After a while, the principal just gave up and let me stay. We came to an agreement that I could stay in the class down the hall and would return when we got a permanent teacher. Eventually we did get a permanent teacher for the remainder of the school year, but I didn't learn too much in 5th grade. I guess the most important thing I learned was that I could get what I wanted if I spoke up.

Now, when I look back, I see how much my attitude toward education has really changed. I learned that I had to open up more if I wanted people to listen to me or help me. But I also think my problems could have easily been avoided if someone had just stopped and listened to me.

I began to work harder, and when I had a test or didn't understand something, I'd ask and ask again until it was made clear to me. I have always known that to make it in the world, you have to have an education. But because I had so much trouble learning, I never thought I could like school.

Soon, my attitude changed. I began to enjoy school because I was able to keep up.

Since I've been in special education, I've found out that I just need to go slower, and I can actually enjoy my work. And now that I've almost finished high school, I think I want to go to college, because I like to learn. I want to learn.

It helps that my mother takes a big interest in my education. I tell her all the time what I am learning in school. She is very proud of what I am doing and helps me out whenever she can. She makes me feel that as long as I try my best, I can do it.

Education is important to me because it will help me find a job, so I can have money to do the things that I enjoy, like going to museums or going shopping. But education is also important because it's fun. I try to learn whatever I can when I'm not in school. I've taken a class on computers every summer since I began high school.

I also go to the library and take out books on writing, poetry, art, history, science fiction, and music. And whenever I can, I go to museums or to the Botanical Garden. Education is more than what you can get out of a textbook in school. It's also what you learn from life.

Zizi was 18 when she wrote this story.
She went on to publish two books.

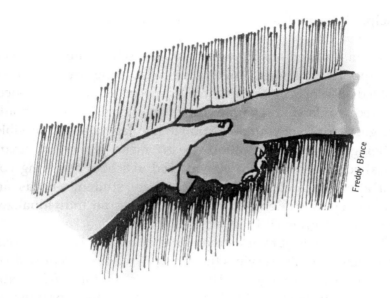

Freddy Bruce

Special Education Is Supposed to Help

By Alice Rosenthal

Special education is supposed to be a helping hand for students who need extra support because they have a learning problem or other disability. But for too many students, special education is more like quicksand: They get stuck in a system that fails to provide the help they need to learn. Statistics show that too few students in special education graduate from high school. Here's more information about special education and how you can get the most out of it:

Special education is a set of services required by federal law for students with disabilities. If you have a disability that affects your learning, such as emotional problems, learning disabilities, or a speech impairment, you can get special education services to help. There are tests to figure out if you have a disability and how severe it is.

If you do need special education, the school must give you the supports you need, preferably right alongside your non-disabled classmates. Unfortunately, special education services are often provided in separate classes or schools. The goal should be to get as much of your education in regular classes as possible.

Being in special education doesn't mean you're not smart. Special education can help you succeed in school by giving you extra attention and support. Since every student's needs are different, every student with a disability has an Individualized Education Program (IEP).

The IEP spells out your strengths and challenges, your educational goals, and the services the school is required to provide to help you reach those goals. That can mean anything from extra tutoring all the way to attending a small, specialized program or school. But wherever you go to school, you still have the right to earn a high school diploma.

By law, schools must do what the IEP says. It's not optional. Also, the law says you must be evaluated (tested) by qualified people who can help decide what you really need to succeed in school. You should be evaluated at least every three years because your needs can change.

Make sure that you understand what's in your IEP and that it is really what you need. If not, speak up! Advocate for yourself, and find teachers, agency staff, guidance counselors, mentors, or other adults who can help explain it and who will speak up for you.

It's also important to tell the adults in your life about your own short- and long-term life goals. These goals are important in creating a good IEP. Under federal law, by at least age 16, you have the right to be involved in your IEP meeting and to help make the plan for your transition to adult life based on your goals. At age 18, in most states, students have the right to make their own decisions regarding their IEP. (In New York, parents or guardians have the right through age 21.)

Every year, there is a meeting to review and update your IEP, based on your progress and needs. At the meeting, your teachers and principal are supposed to show what they're doing to help you reach your IEP goals. It's important to know what the school is supposed to be doing to help you meet your goals.

For too many students, special education is like quicksand: They get stuck in a system that fails to provide the help they need.

The IEP meeting is a good place to make sure you are in the right program and getting the right services. It is also a good time to change your program if it's not working for you or you are not satisfied with it. If your IEP is working for you, great. If not—or if you need more help—reach out to supportive adults at school and at home. Ask for a copy of your IEP, and then ask them to explain the IEP in language you can understand.

Tell them what you're struggling with. They should be able to think of services that will help you—or you may have an idea yourself. Ask them to come to the IEP meeting to give support and to advocate for you.

If the school claims to be providing services that you're not getting, speak up! Don't assume the school will follow the law. Some principals and special education teachers are overloaded, poorly trained, or don't care. Some schools just don't want to spend the time and money on what you deserve.

Finally, if you disagree with your special education services, your parent has due process rights, and you have the right to stay in school until the end of the school year in which you turn 21.

Alice Rosenthal is a staff attorney at Advocates for Children of New York, which works to provide quality public education services for all.

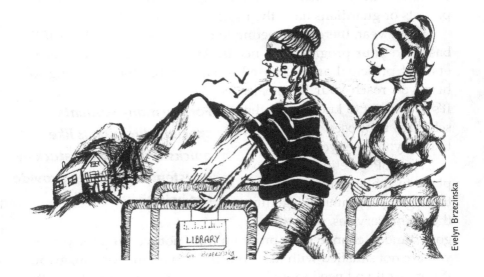

Evelyn Brzezinska

I See the World Through Different Eyes

By Donna Hutchinson

Last summer, I got a job as a counselor at a camp for blind children. When I told people what I was going to be doing, some had blank expressions. Some were good Samaritans who thought it was a nice thing to do. Others gave me strange looks that seemed to say, "Why can't you work with normal people?" This made it seem as though the blind and visually impaired were not people; aliens was more like it. But since I hadn't started working with them yet, I didn't know what to say in their defense.

The Vacation Camp for the Blind and Visually Impaired is located in Spring Valley, NY, about an hour's drive from New York City, where I live. It's a suburban area, with lots of trees and one-family houses. There aren't any streetlights and by 8 p.m. it's pitch dark. If you don't have a car, you're out of luck because stores are miles away.

One unusual thing about the camp is that there are railings throughout the grounds to help the blind campers find their way around. For example, if a camper is leaving the library to go back to her dorm, she walks along holding on to the rails, using them as a guide. Every so often, she will reach an opening in the rail- ing—that means she's reached a dorm or some other building. At that spot, there is some writing in Braille that tells her where she is.

I went up there for the first time in March to get a feel for the place. I met about 20 of the 80 staff people. They greeted me with smiles and I started asking about camp life.

George was 19 and had been a counselor for three summers. He tried to give me an idea of what working there was like: "You have to bathe campers; get up early and go to sleep late; you're constantly on your feet and you don't get paid much." But, he added, "It's nice though, cause you get to bug out and stuff. You just have to see for yourself. You'll like it."

When I returned to the camp in the summer, I was ready to work hard and to have an interesting experience. On the first day, all the new staff members had to participate in the "blindfold activity." This activity gave us a better understanding of what it's like to be blind. First, our eyes were covered with a piece

There are railings throughout the grounds to help the blind campers find their way around.

of cloth. Then we were paired with another staff person who took us on a walk around the camp.

Through this activity, I learned to depend more on my mem- ory and my other senses—especially hearing—since I couldn't see a thing. I also learned to trust others more because I had to depend on the person I was walking with to help me find my way.

As we traveled along the path, I tried to picture where I was going, but it was all dark. I was in complete darkness with no sense of control over my life. It was upsetting not to be able to depend on myself. I was glad to take my blindfold off.

The first set of campers arrived in early July. There were 180 of them, mostly adults between the ages of 25 and 50. The group included couples where one person was blind and the other was not; families where both parents were blind, but not their kids; and families where both parents could see, but their children couldn't.

On a typical day, I got up at 7:30 to be at breakfast at 8. (Part of my job was serving the campers their meals.) For the rest of the morning, I was usually assigned to take the campers on walks, play ball with them, or read them the newspaper.

C amp was different from home. At home, I am accustomed to hanging out with one group of people. We go to the same places and do the same things, talk about the same issues, and worry about the same problems. At camp, I met people of different backgrounds, races, and cultures. The staff members were from all over the world—from Sweden to Ivory Coast, Africa—and all different corners of the United States.

In this environment, I not only learned about others but myself too. I became more culturally aware and open to different views and experiences. Interacting with so many different kinds of people enriched my life.

The campers were a diverse group too. They all had different attitudes about their blindness. Some were born blind and some lost their sight later in life. Some complained about not being able to see, while others accepted it with no fuss or fight.

I talked to them to try to understand their feelings. One camper who had been able to see for much of her life told me, "When I lost my vision, it was very hard to deal with it. In the beginning, I cried many nights, and even wanted to kill myself. My family and friends talked to me many times, and through them I finally realized, 'I can't fight my blindness. That's the way I am. Crying about it won't change anything.' I finally accepted it."

I became close to Anna, a visually impaired counselor. She was a 20-year-old college student from Utah. At the beginning of the summer we worked together, waiting table at meals.

While the campers ate, we sat casually talking about food, work, and guys. We had a lot of laughs, and it was nice working alongside her. Partway through the summer, our job assignments were changed. We were working on opposite sides of the dining hall and seldom saw each other.

I missed her because it was much easier when Anna and I worked as a team. She would get the bread, I'd put on the butter. She'd pour the coffee, I'd add the milk and the sugar. Now, I worked by myself with nine impatient campers all screaming my name at the same time. "Donna, I need another sandwich." "Donna, I need some coffee." "Donna, I need a slice of bread."

Even though there were difficult moments, I enjoyed working with the blind and visually impaired. I liked talking to them about concerns they had or just giving directions around camp. I also enjoyed having responsibilities and being trusted to do my job.

The one bad thing was that I didn't have time to myself. I couldn't read my book for as long as I wanted, get up as late or listen to music as loud. At home, I decide whether to do work around the house or just be idle. At camp, I had to work whether I felt like it or not.

I plan to continue working with visually impaired people in the future. It's something I enjoy and get satisfaction from doing. I believe the disabled are entitled to everything the rest of us are, and doing what I can do to help them get their share makes me feel good.

Toward the end of the summer, I learned another, sadder lesson. Anna and I were back together, waiting the same table again. I was happy because I wasn't constantly on my feet.

Since we would be going home shortly, we spoke about our plans for the fall. Anna was going back to college, her loved ones, and the state of Utah. I was excited to go home because I had summer reading and research assignments to do before school started.

Then, the morning before the last campers went home, Anna came into the dining hall late, rubbing her eyes with her fingers. "What's the matter?" I asked. "My eyes," she said. "It's like...I can't see. Everything is like it's foggy."

Even though she's had problems with her eyes, before that morning, she could see pretty well. "Did you get any sleep last night?" I asked. (We had all been on duty and didn't get to bed until a couple hours later than usual.) "Don't worry," I said, thinking her eyes were just tired. "It will go away and you'll feel better in no time."

One camper told me, "I finally realized, I can't fight my blindness. That's the way I am."

That morning Anna didn't eat anything. She looked terrible, leaning against the wall in the dining room. I told her to sit, and I'd wait on the table. After breakfast, I didn't see her to say good-bye. I didn't think much of it because we had plans to meet and take pictures later in the day. I left and went to take one of the campers to his morning activities.

Anna didn't show up for lunch. I asked other counselors if they had seen her, but nobody had. As I was about to ask some-one else, a supervisor who was walking by called me and a few other counselors aside. He said, "Anna lost all her remaining sight. She is in the hospital undergoing surgery and we're going to have to be there to help her through it."

I thought, "How can Anna lose her sight? Just yesterday we were all merry and planning to take pictures of each other. How could this happen to her? She was so nice, friendly, and caring. Why her of all people? She didn't do anything wrong."

This incident really taught me something: we should live day by day. After all, we never know what tomorrow holds. We could be shot dead, get hit by a car, or suddenly go blind.

Donna was 16 when she wrote this story.
She later went to college and graduate school and
became a middle school teacher.

Fernando Mendez

My Uncle's Chair

By Tonya Leslie

My uncle was 25 when he died. I was 8. I used to think he and I were the same age. He couldn't walk and he couldn't talk. He couldn't even move. He would just sit in the back room of my grandmother's house and watch TV all day long. Sometimes I wondered if he understood what he was watching or if he even cared.

He had cerebral palsy. I never understood what that meant. All I knew was that he couldn't run and play, that he couldn't sit with us and eat at the dinner table, and that he wasn't able to take care of himself.

I never thought of him as being crippled. In fact, I never really thought about it at all. Sometimes it's hard to think about things you never really understand in the first place. To other people he was different but to me he was my uncle and he was normal.

I would go into the back room and talk to him sometimes. I would do flips and jumps on the bed and he would laugh and laugh. Sometimes I would do it when Gran was feeding him and she would get mad at me because she didn't want him to choke.

I would do it anyway because I wanted him to laugh. I wanted him to be happy because I didn't think he was happy sitting in his chair all day.

Gran was a nurse. She took care of him all the time. She fed him, cleaned him, and tried to make him happy. She would sing to him while he ate and tell him stories about my sister, my baby cousin, and me.

I was surprised at how much my uncle, who never once spoke to me, added to my life.

Grandad would take him out to the beach with us. He would sit him in a beach chair, and my uncle would laugh while my sister and I jumped in the waves. My baby cousin would laugh too, even though she didn't know why.

My uncle's presence was constant and I took him for granted. I thought that whenever I went to my grandparent's house, he would be there, in the back room, sitting in his chair.

When I found out he died, I cried. Everyone said that he was in a better place, that he was in God's home where there is no pain. I hoped for his sake that it was true.

After the funeral I went in his room and sat in his chair. I had never sat there before. I looked at the room the way he must have seen it all those years. The TV was still in its place and the shades were open. The sun warmed the room, but in the chair I felt cold and lonely.

I thought about him and was surprised at how much my uncle, who never once spoke to me, added to my life. I prayed that where he was now he could run and jump, that he could do

all the things he had watched me do for so many years.
And I also hoped that he knew that I loved him.

---

*Tonya was 18 when she wrote this story. After college,
she earned a graduate degree in education from New York
University and worked in educational publishing.*

Kat Morris

I Can Do It Myself

By Tania Morales

When a country struggles for independence, its people fight for their rights and freedom. My fight for independence is from all the people who want to help me because I'm disabled. Sadly, I fight with family to make them understand my need to be more independent. I can't be—and I don't want to be—depending on everyone around me all the time.

I have Frederick's ataxia, which is a genetic disease (I was born with it). As the disease develops, it makes walking, speech, and hand control more difficult. I was diagnosed five years ago and I started using a wheelchair about four years ago.

I'm still trying to deal with having this disease. It hurts me that I can't move around and do things like I used to do. Until I was 13, I had fun with my friends, running around, racing bikes and dancing. But ataxia affects the nerves and muscles and makes it hard to walk. My handwriting and speech aren't as steady as they used to be, either.

Since there's no cure or treatment to stop this disease, I'll have to live with it until I die. It is going to get worse with time. So it's important to me to be able to control my life now, while I can.

I need to be independent to be able to survive in this world and also just to feel normal. I want to be like other teens. That includes doing things on my own, away from my family and other adults looking after me. Being independent allows me to not even think of myself as disabled.

I don't like asking for help because I don't like to bother people. At home I'm usually asking someone to pass me things I need, like my notebooks or something to drink or eat.

I live on the second floor of a house and if I want to go out, I have to ask someone to take me down because I can't do it on my own. I have to be carried up or down the stairs on my sisters' or brothers' backs because there isn't an elevator.

My fight for independence is from all the people who want to help me because I'm disabled.

I told my family that it would be better if we found a more accessible apartment or house so that I wouldn't have to bother them. But they tell me we can't move now, and say, "Helping you is not a bother."

I say to myself, "Yes it is," because sometimes when I ask for something, I have to wait five minutes or more until they can stop what they're doing to get what I need. And I can't be easy to carry now that I'm adult-sized. Constantly asking for help makes me frustrated and sad because I remember that I was once able to do what I wanted by myself.

Most of the time, if I want to go somewhere other than school, I have to ask someone, like my mom or sister, to drive me. Sometimes I take the Access-A-Ride, which is a van that takes you door-to-door anywhere you want to go within the New York City area. The "cheese bus" (a short yellow school bus) takes me back and forth from school.

At Brooklyn International High School, I'm supposed to have a "para" with me all the time. A para (short for paraprofessional) is a person who is paid by the government to take care of disabled kids at school. This person is supposed to take notes for me, push me around school, and help me go to the bathroom.

I'm glad to have help when I need it, but it's really annoying to have someone next to me all the time in school even though I'm still able to do most of the school work by myself. When the para is with me, I can't have a private conversation with my friends or go off with them down the hall.

Sometimes there isn't a para available. It's really cool because I can have fun and talk with my friends without an adult hanging around. And the other students love to take me around.

I want to do things like other teens. Growing up, I wanted to be a dancer or an astronomer. When I got sick, I had to stop dancing, but I still follow astronomy.

*I*n the summer of 2003, I applied for the American Museum of Natural History's astronomy program for teens. When I got the acceptance letter, I was so happy. I only thought of going there and meeting other teens with the same passion as me.

But about a week before the program started, my mom said, "I will go with you and make sure that you are going to be in good hands."

"Mom, you can't go with me!" I said, but she insisted. She went with me on the Access-A-Ride and stayed the entire day. I was so angry because I wanted to go there by myself to show that even though I was in a wheelchair, I could do it.

Afterward I argued with her. "You're not giving me the space and the responsibility of growing up," I said, and I kept repeating my point of view. I was so happy when, two weeks into the program, I convinced her to let me go by myself on the Access-A-Ride.

When I was with my mom, no one else in the program got near me. But on my own I had so much fun, because everyone wanted to push me. It was different from family or a paid para pushing me because they were my age and it was all part of having fun.

But the Access-A-Ride came to pick me up from the museum nearly an hour late, and my mom was so worried that she came with me the next day.

I tried arguing again. I explained, "That one day you let me go by myself, I really enjoyed it. I want to have another day like that." I told her I really wanted to taste independence. But no—even though she didn't go with me, she sent my sister or my nephew to take care of me.

So I knew I'd have another battle when my school sent me to an internship last February.

I informed Mom that I was going to have two internships, one at the Prospect Park Zoo and another one here at Youth Communication. Since I was still doing the museum's astronomy program, I was going to travel a lot.

Sure enough, she said, "I'll go with you."

We argued about it for days. I understood that she was worried. In addition to her usual concerns, I had just had surgery and she didn't want me to overwork.

But by the time the internships started, I had convinced her that I could go by myself. I told her how I was going to get there and she bought me a cell phone so I could call her and tell her where I was and that I was OK.

At first I used Access-A-Ride. But since Youth Communication is in Manhattan, like the museum, I thought that I could take a regular city bus to go from there to the museum. I spent a good afternoon looking through bus maps over the Internet for the easiest way to get to the museum.

It felt so cool taking the bus to the museum by myself. I felt free and able to do anything I wanted. I felt like I was just another normal teen and even forgot about being sick. It was fun to be on my own and be a part of the city, seeing so many people shopping, getting out of work, or just hanging around.

I t hasn't always been easy getting around by myself, especially if it is snowing or raining. Crossing streets can be a little difficult when the streets aren't in good shape or are under construction. Sometimes the wheels get cold and freeze my hands. Sometimes I've got to roll through puddles on the street corners. But usually there is a police officer or someone else who helps me go across.

Taking the bus to the museum by myself, I felt free and able to do anything I wanted. I felt like just another normal teen.

I know my mom worries about me. I love her very much and it hurts when we argue. But she doesn't understand that I need to be independent and that it feels like a burden to have everyone worrying about me. I know what I'm doing and I know I can do it.

One of the most difficult battles I've had for independence concerned the para. This fall, I decided that I didn't want a para with me. But I had to convince both my family and my school's principal that I'd be fine without one.

The principal was the easy part. It turned out that she thought it was a great idea for me to become more independent. But she also knew that my mom wouldn't want me to be without the para.

It was up to me to convince my mom. She feared that something bad could happen to me while I went from class to class and wanted someone with me all the time because I'd only been wheeling myself in the wheelchair for a year or so.

I talked and talked to my mom. I even cried because I felt hurt that she didn't trust my strength. Even worse, I feared that maybe she was hiding something from me, like additional problems with my health. The thought that I could never do things or go places myself again was destroying the little light I had.

Eventually, my mother said that I could try not having a para at school. It feels wonderful to be able to play and hang out with my friends. Pushing myself in school is a form of physical therapy, too, because I work out with my hands. My arms are still getting used to pushing with a lot of force, but it's good exercise and I'm getting arm muscles!

Now I want to go out of state for college. My mom is like, "I'll go with you!" But she says it jokingly. She believes I'm able to do things. Even though she is afraid, I think she knows I'll be OK. I've been able to succeed at everything I've been through one way or another. I have discovered that the world is full of adventures, and to enjoy them, the first step was to fight for my independence.

Tania was 18 when she wrote this story. She attended John Jay College and majored in computer information systems and public information.

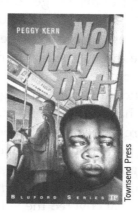

Townsend Press

No Way Out

Harold Davis took a deep breath and slowly started to peel the gauze from the wound on his grandmother's leg.

"Hold on, Grandma. I'm almost done," he said quietly.

"Don't worry, baby. It doesn't hurt too much," she replied, wincing slightly. "Just take your time."

Harold glanced up at his grandmother lying on the couch. He could tell she was in pain from the way she gripped the cushions, but still she managed to smile back at him.

"Go ahead, child. Really, it's okay," she insisted.

Harold gently peeled away the sticky gauze and looked at the large, swollen wound. It was blood red, with a white film along the edges.

It looks angry, Harold thought as he carefully spread ointment over the cut and covered it with a clean bandage. He hated looking at her leg, but he knew he had no choice. It was her first day out of the hospital, and she needed his help.

Here's the first chapter from No Way Out, by Peggy Kern, a novel about a teen struggling to take care of his disabled grandmother. No Way Out is one of several books in the Bluford Series™ by Townsend Press.

"Okay Grandma, all done. I'll get dinner started," Harold said as he turned the television to her favorite channel and put away her medical supplies. "Those bandages the hospital gave us are cheap. We need the more expensive kind that won't stick so much. Like the doctor said."

"Oh Harold," Grandma sighed, struggling to sit up on the couch. "I'm sorry you have to do all this for me. But don't you worry. Just a few more weeks, and I'll be good as new." She smoothed out her long floral housedress and fussed with her hair as she talked. "Just as good as new."

"I know, Grandma," he said, forcing himself not to stare at the deep purple bruise that covered the left side of her forehead. He wanted her words to be true, but after the events of the last few days, he wasn't sure. Grandma had turned seventy-three last month, and today she seemed even older.

At least she's home again, he thought to himself. At least we're home.

Two days ago, Grandma fell on the front steps of their apartment building, banging her head on the pavement, spraining her ankle, and cutting her leg badly. Mr. Harris, their neighbor, had found her lying on the sidewalk and called an ambulance. He'd also driven to Bluford High, where Harold was a freshman, to take him to the hospital. Harold shuddered as the events of that day flashed in his mind like a nightmare.

He had been in the middle of Ms. Webb's algebra class when Ms. Spencer, the school principal, rushed into his classroom.

"Harold, I need you in the office," she said, her voice tense. "Now."

Everyone in the class turned to face him.

"Boy, don't tell me you're in trouble. You don't do nothin' wrong," said Rodney Banks.

"Maybe he broke into the cafeteria. Look at his stomach. You know that boy likes to eat," added Andre Jenkins with a smirk. Harold cringed in embarrassment.

"Man, leave him alone," snapped Darrell Mercer, Harold's

friend. "This ain't any of your business."

"That's enough, gentlemen!" warned Ms. Webb as Harold left the classroom.

When Harold arrived at the principal's office, Mr. Harris was standing at the counter, quietly arguing with Ms. Bader, the school secretary.

Why's he here? Harold wondered.

Mr. Harris lived in the small apartment at the end of their hallway. He'd moved in a few months ago, though in that time, Harold had hardly said a word to him.

"I'm sorry, but you're not on the list, Mr. Harris. We cannot let you drive Harold to the hospital," Ms. Bader explained.

Mr. Harris's eyes were focused and determined. "I understand," he replied calmly. "But his grandmother asked me to come. She doesn't want him to be scared."

"I'm sure that's true, but I can't change school policy, Mr. Harris—"

"What happened?" Harold asked, interrupting them. "What happened to Grandma?"

The office suddenly grew silent. Harold saw the concern on Ms. Bader's face, but before she could reply, Mr. Harris stepped forward, putting his hand on Harold's shoulder. A thin streak of dried blood stained his sleeve. Harold's heart raced.

"It's all right. She's all right," Mr. Harris said calmly. "She fell down and banged herself up pretty bad, but I've seen worse. She's at the hospital now. Your teachers are going to take you over there right now," he said, glancing back at Ms. Bader and Ms. Spencer. "I'll be right behind you."

At the hospital, Harold sat for hours beneath the buzzing fluorescent lights of the crowded waiting room. Doctors hurried back and forth. Families wandered in and out, some in tears. He needed to use the bathroom, but he didn't want to get up in case the doctors came looking for him.

Finally, well after sunset, a doctor sat next to him and described what happened. Harold felt dizzy when the doctor began explaining the details of Grandma's condition.

Significant leg abrasion and minor head trauma.

Diabetes, obesity, and age complicate her injuries.

Slow recovery. Constant care may be required.

Harold stared at the floor, his head throbbing at the news. After the doctor left, he was visited by a social worker, a young woman with neat hair and lipstick and shoes that clicked on the floor as she walked. She asked Harold questions that haunted him ever since.

"Do you have any other family, Harold? Is there someone you can stay with?"

She paused, waiting for him to answer. Harold stared at the dirty flecks in the tile floor.

"If not, we'll need to place you somewhere while your grandmother—"

"No! I'm staying here!" he insisted, jumping out of his chair and backing away from her like an animal about to be trapped. "I'm staying with Grandma." He knew he sounded like a child, but he couldn't help it.

He was shaking with panic, his heart pounding frantically as the full meaning of her words sank in. There was no other family. His mom died in childbirth with him, and his father had run out shortly after that. He had no one else to stay with. His eyes burned with tears, and he looked around desperately. He thought he might throw up, right there on the hospital floor.

Just then, Mr. Harris stepped forward. Had he been there the entire time? Harold couldn't recall. The evening had been a blur.

"The boy can stay with me tonight, ma'am," Mr. Harris said quietly. "I live just up the hall from his apartment. I'm sure Mrs. Davis will give her consent."

Harold stayed at Mr. Harris's that evening and the next, sleeping on a foldout sofa at night and visiting Grandma at the hospital all day. Though just two days passed since Grandma fell, their apartment felt like a foreign place to Harold when they returned.

Normally it was filled with the aroma of his grandmother's cooking. But when Harold unlocked the door and helped Grandma in, it smelled stale and musty. He knew he'd need to clean it, but first he had to cook dinner.

Harold poked around the fridge. The milk was already start- ing to sour. There weren't enough eggs for tomorrow's breakfast. Fortunately, Mr. Harris had dropped off a tray of lasagna. Harold took it out of the refrigerator and put it in the stove, turning it to 350 degrees as Mr. Harris said. Then he returned to the living room to check on Grandma.

The usually clean living room was now cluttered with ban- dages, unanswered mail and the bulky wooden crutches from the hospital. Pillows were piled awkwardly on the couch to keep Grandma's ankle elevated. A bag of dirty laundry sat in the cor- ner where she left it two days ago, still waiting to be washed.

"My goodness, this place is a mess," Grandma said, almost to herself. "Now, don't you worry about all this, Harold. I just need to rest up for a little while and we'll be back to our normal schedule. Don't you forget about your homework, either," she added. "I might need to stay off this leg for a few weeks, but that don't mean I won't be checking on you."

"Yes, Grandma," he replied, rubbing his temples. He could feel a dull headache starting to build behind his eyes.

School's the least of my worries now, Grandma, he wanted to say. Dishes needed to be washed. Laundry needed to be done. The bathroom needed scrubbing. Groceries needed to be bought. And more than anything, Grandma needed his help.

"Do you have any other family, Harold? Is there someone you can stay with?" The social worker's questions echoed in his mind again. Harold shuddered, his headache worsening.

Harold rummaged through the cabinets for some clean din- ner plates. Unless he was hungry, he rarely came into the kitchen. He spent most of his time in the living room watching television or doing his homework at their small table. The kitchen was Grandma's territory, and Harold felt lost among the pots and pans and plastic containers of flour, spices, and odd foods he could not identify. There were shelves of canned peaches and sweet potatoes, which she would use to make pies.

Was she still allowed to eat pie? he wondered.

The hospital had sent them home with a list of "approved" foods for his grandmother, but he hadn't had a chance to read the list yet. Harold didn't really understand her diabetes. She'd had the disease for a long time and it never seemed to be a problem before. But at the hospital, her doctors discovered some sores on her feet when they examined her. They said she could have "complications" if she didn't control her weight and diet.

Harold found the dinner plates piled in the sink. He washed two plates and checked on Mr. Harris's lasagna. After five minutes in the oven, it was still cool, especially in the middle.

"Grandma," he called, turning up the oven dial to 400 degrees. "How long does it take to heat up lasagna?"

There was no reply.

"Grandma?" he repeated, waiting for a response that didn't come. "Grandma?"

He rushed into the living room, his heart suddenly pounding. His grandmother lay still, asleep on the couch. Her head leaned to one side, and her chest rose and fell heavily with each breath. He could see the swollen bruise on her forehead and the bandage peeking out from beneath her long dress. It was already turning brown, even though he just changed the dressing. He turned off the television and covered her with a blanket—what she usually did for him when he was sick.

"How are we gonna get through this, Grandma?" he whispered as he leaned over her, gently kissing her forehead. "Who's gonna make dinner while your leg heals?" Harold swallowed hard, and stood up.

What if it doesn't? he wondered.

Harold's head throbbed now. He was hungry and exhausted, and he didn't want to think any more. He ate a piece of Mr. Harris's lukewarm lasagna and washed the dishes. Then he grabbed a pillow and blanket from his bedroom and sat on the floor by the couch.

The apartment was silent, except for his grandmother's breathing and the occasional siren outside.

"Do you have any other family, Harold? Is there someone you can stay with?"

In the dark apartment, the questions crashed down on him in endless waves.

"There's no one else," he whispered into the darkness. "We're alone."

If you'd like to continue reading this book, it is available for $1/copy from TownsendPress.com. Or tell an adult (like your teacher) that they can receive copies of *No Way Out* for free if they order a class set of 15 or more copies of *Different But Equal*. To order, call 212-279-0708 x115 or visit www.youthcomm.org.

Teens:
How to Get More Out of This Book

Self-help: The teens who wrote the stories in this book did so because they hope that telling their stories will help readers who are facing similar challenges. They want you to know that you are not alone, and that taking specific steps can help you manage or overcome very difficult situations. They've done their best to be clear about the actions that worked for them so you can see if they'll work for you.

Writing: You can also use the book to improve your writing skills. Each teen in this book wrote 5-10 drafts of his or her story before it was published. If you read the stories closely you'll see that the teens work to include a beginning, a middle, and an end, and good scenes, description, dialogue, and anecdotes (little stories). To improve your writing, take a look at how these writers construct their stories. Try some of their techniques in your own writing.

Reading: Finally, you'll notice that we include the first chapter from a Bluford Series novel in this book, alongside the true stories by teens. We hope you'll like it enough to continue reading. The more you read, the more you'll strengthen your reading skills. Teens at Youth Communication like the Bluford novels because they explore themes similar to those in their own stories. Your school may already have the Bluford books. If not, you can order them online for only $1.

Resources on the Web

We will occasionally post Think About It questions on our website, www.youthcomm.org, to accompany stories in this and other Youth Communication books. We try out the questions with teens and post the ones they like best. Many teens report that writing answers to those questions in a journal is very helpful.

How to Use This Book in Staff Training

Staff say that reading these stories gives them greater insight into what teens are thinking and feeling, and new strategies for working with them. You can help the staff you work with by using these stories as case studies.

Select one story to read in the group, and ask staff to identify and discuss the main issue facing the teen. There may be disagreement about this, based on the background and experience of staff. That is fine. One point of the exercise is that teens have complex lives and needs. Adults can probably be more effective if they don't focus too narrowly and can see several dimensions of their clients.

Ask staff: What issues or feelings does the story provoke in them? What kind of help do they think the teen wants? What interventions are likely to be most promising? Least effective? Why? How would you build trust with the teen writer? How have other adults failed the teen, and how might that affect his or her willingness to accept help? What other resources would be helpful to this teen, such as peer support, a mentor, counseling, family therapy, etc?

Resources on the Web

From time to time we will post Think About It questions on our website, www.youthcomm.org, to accompany stories in this and other Youth Communication books. We try out the questions with teens and post the ones that they find most effective. We'll also post lessons for some of the stories. Adults can use the questions and lessons in workshops.

Discussion Guide

Teachers and Staff:
How to Use This Book in Groups

When working with teens individually or in groups, you can use these stories to help young people face difficult issues in a way that feels safe to them. That's because talking about the issues in the stories usually feels safer to teens than talking about those same issues in their own lives. Addressing issues through the stories allows for some personal distance; they hit close to home, but not too close. Talking about them opens up a safe place for reflection. As teens gain confidence talking about the issues in the stories, they usually become more comfortable talking about those issues in their own lives.

Below are general questions to guide your discussion. In most cases you can read a story and conduct a discussion in one 45-minute session. Teens are usually happy to read the stories aloud, with each teen reading a paragraph or two. (Allow teens to pass if they don't want to read.) It takes 10-15 minutes to read a story straight through. However, it is often more effective to let workshop participants make comments and discuss the story as you go along. The workshop leader may even want to annotate her copy of the story beforehand with key questions.

If teens read the story ahead of time or silently, it's good to break the ice with a few questions that get everyone on the same page: Who is the main character? How old is she? What happened to her? How did she respond? Another good starting question is: "What stood out for you in the story?" Go around the room and let each person briefly mention one thing.

Then move on to open-ended questions, which encourage participants to think more deeply about what the writers were feeling, the choices they faced, and the actions they took. There are no right or wrong answers to the open-ended questions.

Open-ended questions encourage participants to think about how the themes, emotions, and choices in the stories relate to their own lives. Here are some examples of open-ended questions that we have found to be effective. You can use variations of these questions with almost any story in this book.

—What main problem or challenge did the writer face?

—What choices did the teen have in trying to deal with the problem?

—Which way of dealing with the problem was most effective for the teen? Why?

—What strengths, skills, or resources did the teen use to address the challenge?

—If you were in the writer's shoes, what would you have done?

—What could adults have done better to help this young person?

—What have you learned by reading this story that you didn't know before?

—What, if anything, will you do differently after reading this story?

—What surprised you in this story?

—Do you have a different view of this issue, or see a different way of dealing with it, after reading this story? Why or why not?

Credits

The stories in this book originally appeared in the following Youth Communication publications:

"The Art of Shotokan" by Otis Hampton, *Represent*, Fall 2011; "Struggling With a Learning Disability" by Sarah B., *New Youth Connections*, December 1992; "Facing Reality" by Tania Morales, *New Youth Connections*, May/June 2004; "What's It Like Being Blind?" by Slade Anderson, *New Youth Connections*, June 1993; "Mainstreaming: Making It in the Real World" by Slade Anderson, *New Youth Connections*, June 1993; "Tongue Tied" by Joanna Fu, *New Youth Connections*, November 1999; "My Sister's Keeper" by Anonymous, *New Youth Connections*, April 2009; "Deaf but Not Dumb" by Oni Nicolarakis, *New Youth Connections*, September/October 1997; "No Such Thing As Normal" by Fabio Botarelli, *New Youth Connections*, January/February 2006; "Getting the Words Out" by Gamal Jones, *New Youth Connections*, January/February 2007; "Why People Stutter" by Gamal Jones, *New Youth Connections*, January/February 2007; "Will the Tortoise Win the Race?" by Eric Green, *Represent*, March/April 2005; "A Classmate in a Wheelchair" by Esther Rajavelu, *New Youth Connections*, September/October 1995; "From Sore Loser to MVP" by Michelle Stallworth, *New Youth Connections*, May/June 1996; "Tongue-Tied" by Donald Moore, *New Youth Connections*, March 2007; "Listen, and I'll Learn," by Zizi Lavada Baity, *New Youth Connections*, April 1998; "Special Education Is Supposed to Help," by Alice Rosenthal, *Represent*, March/April 2009; "I See the World Through Different Eyes" by Donna Hutchinson, *New Youth Connections*, April 1995; "My Uncle's Chair" by Tonya Leslie, *New Youth Connections*, May 1990; "I Can Do It Myself" by Tania Morales, *New Youth Connections*, January/February 2005.

About
Youth Communication

Youth Communication, founded in 1980, is a nonprofit youth development program located in New York City whose mission is to teach writing, journalism, and leadership skills. The teenagers we train become writers for our websites and books and for two print magazines: *New Youth Connections*, a general-interest youth magazine, and *Represent*, a magazine by and for young people in foster care.

Each year, up to 100 young people participate in Youth Communication's school-year and summer journalism workshops, where they work under the direction of full-time professional editors. Most are African-American, Latino, or Asian, and many are recent immigrants. The opportunity to reach their peers with accurate portrayals of their lives and important self-help information motivates the young writers to create powerful stories.

Our goal is to run a strong youth development program in which teens produce high quality stories that inform and inspire their peers. Doing so requires us to be sensitive to the complicated lives and emotions of the teen participants while also providing an intellectually rigorous experience. We achieve that goal in the writing/teaching/editing relationship, which is the core of our program.

Our teaching and editorial process begins with discussions

between adult editors and the teen staff. In those meetings, the teens and the editors work together to identify the most important issues in the teens' lives and to figure out how those issues can be turned into stories that will resonate with teen readers.

Once story topics are chosen, students begin the process of crafting their stories. For a personal story, that means revisiting events in one's past to understand their significance for the future. For a commentary, it means developing a logical and persuasive point of view. For a reported story, it means gathering information through research and interviews. Students look inward and outward as they try to make sense of their experiences and the world around them and find the points of intersection between personal and social concerns. That process can take a few weeks or a few months. Stories frequently go through 10 or more drafts as students work under the guidance of their editors, the way any professional writer does.

Many of the students who walk through our doors have uneven skills, as a result of poor education, living under extremely stressful conditions, or coming from homes where English is a second language. Yet, to complete their stories, students must successfully perform a wide range of activities, including writing and rewriting, reading, discussion, reflection, research, interviewing, and typing. They must work as members of a team and they must accept individual responsibility. They learn to provide constructive criticism, and to accept it. They engage in explorations of truthfulness, fairness, and accuracy. They meet deadlines. They must develop the audacity to believe that they have something important to say and the humility to recognize that saying it well is not a process of instant gratification. Rather, it usually requires a long, hard struggle through many discussions and much rewriting.

It would be impossible to teach these skills and dispositions as separate, disconnected topics, like grammar, ethics, or assertiveness. However, we find that students make rapid progress when they are learning skills in the context of an inquiry that is personally significant to them and that will benefit their peers.

When teens publish their stories—in *New Youth Connections* and *Represent,* on the Web, and in other publications—they reach tens of thousands of teen and adult readers. Teachers, counselors, social workers, and other adults circulate the stories to young people in their classes and out-of-school youth programs. Adults tell us that teens in their programs—including many who are ordinarily resistant to reading—clamor for the stories. Teen readers report that the stories give them information they can't get anywhere else, and inspire them to reflect on their lives and open lines of communication with adults.

Writers usually participate in our program for one semester, though some stay much longer. Years later, many of them report that working here was a turning point in their lives—that it helped them acquire the confidence and skills that they needed for success in college and careers. Scores of our graduates have overcome tremendous obstacles to become journalists, writers, and novelists. They include National Book Award finalist and MacArthur Fellowship winner Edwidge Danticat, novelist Ernesto Quiñonez, writer Veronica Chambers, and *New York Times* reporter Rachel Swarns. Hundreds more are working in law, business, and other careers. Many are teachers, principals, and youth workers, and several have started nonprofit youth programs themselves and work as mentors—helping another generation of young people develop their skills and find their voices.

Youth Communication is a nonprofit educational corporation. Contributions are gratefully accepted and are tax deductible to the fullest extent of the law.

To make a contribution, or for information about our publications and programs, including our catalog of over 100 books and curricula for hard-to-reach teens, see www.youthcomm.org.

About the Editors

Virginia Vitzthum is an editor at *Represent*, Youth Communication's magazine by and for teens in foster care. Before working at Youth Communication she wrote a book about Internet dating and a column for the web magazine salon.com. She's also written for *Ms.*, *Elle*, *the Village Voice*, *Time Out New York*, *Washington City Paper*, and other publications. She has edited law books as well as books about substance abuse treatment and health care policy newsletters. She's written a play and a screenplay; produced several short videos; and volunteered at the 52nd St. Project, a children's theater, where she helped 9- to 11-year-olds write plays.

Keith Hefner co-founded Youth Communication in 1980 and has directed it ever since. He is the recipient of the Luther P. Jackson Education Award from the New York Association of Black Journalists and a MacArthur Fellowship. He was also a Revson Fellow at Columbia University.

Laura Longhine is the editorial director at Youth Communication. She edited *Represent*, Youth Communication's magazine by and for youth in foster care, for three years, and has written for a variety of publications. She has a BA in English from Tufts University and an MS in Journalism from Columbia University.

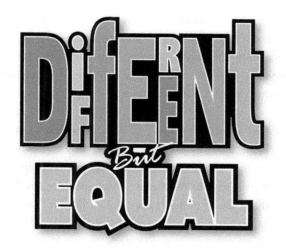

More Helpful Books
From Youth Communication

The Struggle to Be Strong: True Stories by Teens About Overcoming Tough Times. Foreword by Veronica Chambers. Help young people identify and build on their own strengths with 30 personal stories about resiliency. (Free Spirit)

Starting With "I": Personal Stories by Teenagers. "Who am I and who do I want to become?" Thirty-five stories examine this question through the lens of race, ethnicity, gender, sexuality, family, and more. Increase this book's value with the free Teacher's Guide, available from youthcomm.org. (Youth Communication)

Real Stories, Real Teens. Inspire teens to read and recognize their strengths with this collection of 26 true stories by teens. The young writers describe how they overcame significant challenges and stayed true to themselves. Also includes the first chapters from three novels in the Bluford Series. (Youth Communication)

The Courage to Be Yourself: True Stories by Teens About Cliques, Conflicts, and Overcoming Peer Pressure. In 26 first-person stories, teens write about their lives with searing honesty. These stories will inspire young readers to reflect on their own lives, work through their problems, and help them discover who they really are. (Free Spirit)

Out With It: Gay and Straight Teens Write About Homosexuality. Break stereotypes and provide support with this unflinching look at gay life from a teen's perspective. With a focus on urban youth, this book also includes several heterosexual teens' transformative experiences with gay peers. (Youth Communication)

 *Things Get Hectic: Teens Write About the Violence That Surrounds Them.* Violence is commonplace in many teens' lives, be it bullying, gangs, dating, or family relationships. Hear the experiences of victims, perpetrators, and witnesses through more than 50 real-world stories. (Youth Communication)

From Dropout to Achiever: Teens Write About School. Help teens overcome the challenges of graduating, which may involve overcoming family problems, bouncing back from a bad semester, or even dropping out for a time. These teens show how they achieve academic success. (Youth Communication)

 My Secret Addiction: Teens Write About Cutting. These true accounts of cutting, or self-mutilation, offer a window into the personal and family situations that lead to this secret habit, and show how teens can get the help they need. (Youth Communication)

Sticks and Stones: Teens Write About Bullying. Shed light on bullying, as told from the perspectives of the bully, the victim, and the witness. These stories show why bullying occurs, the harm it causes, and how it might be prevented. (Youth Communication)

 Boys to Men: Teens Write About Becoming a Man. The young men in this book write about confronting the challenges of growing up. Their honesty and courage make them role models for teens who are bombarded with contradictory messages about what it means to be a man. (Youth Communication)

Through Thick and Thin: Teens Write About Obesity, Eating Disorders, and Self Image. Help teens who struggle with obesity, eating disorders, and body weight issues. These stories show the pressures teens face when they are confronted by unrealistic standards for physical appearance, and how emotions can affect the way we eat. (Youth Communication)

To order these and other books, go to:
www.youthcomm.org
or call 212-279-0708 x115

CPSIA information can be obtained
at www.ICGtesting.com
Printed in the USA
LVHW021527150222
711208LV00010B/803